T0300674

SO TELL ME
WHAT YOU
WANT

SO TELL ME WHAT YOU WANT

My story of making it in the mad,
bad and fab pop music industry

Nicki Chapman

with Sarah Thompson

SPHERE

SPHERE

First published in Great Britain in 2024 by Sphere

3 5 7 9 10 8 6 4 2

A CIP catalogue record for this book
is available from the British Library.

ISBN 978-1-4087-3230-4

Typeset in Dante by M Rules
Printed and bound in Great Britain by
Clays Ltd, Elcograf S.p.A.

Papers used by Sphere are from well-managed forests
and other responsible sources.

Sphere
An imprint of
Little, Brown Book Group
Carmelite House
50 Victoria Embankment
London EC4Y 0DZ

An Hachette UK Company
www.hachette.co.uk

www.littlebrown.co.uk

To everyone who tried their best, who followed a dream and who believes in being good, honest, dependable and true. There are lots of us.

plugger, n.

A person who promotes pop songs
or other products

OXFORD ENGLISH DICTIONARY

Author's note

Everything in this book is written with love, passion and gratitude to the music industry and everyone in it. Without the start this wonderful business gave me I wouldn't be where I am today. Some of the dates might be a bit hazy and I may not have everything in the right order. But every story in these pages really happened and everyone in it is real.

1

The Winner Takes It All

It's a cold February night in London's Wembley Park and I'm sitting in a hot television studio, in front of a stage, on a little blue sofa. I've been to Wembley plenty of times of course, but tonight I'm here under rather different circumstances. It's the final show of *Pop Idol*, and tonight's the night that we finally get to find out who has won the nation's heart, and a rather lucrative record deal.

It's not a big sofa, as I say, and I'm wedged in here between the record executive Simon Cowell, who has his arm slung round the back of the sofa in a way that suggests we are all in his living room not on live television, and the loveable rogue and radio presenter Neil 'Dr' Fox. The legendary pop producer Pete Waterman is on the other side of Neil. He's so excitable, like a mad professor at times. I adore him. If you don't know me, or what I do, you'd be forgiven for imagining that I'm the token woman, here to make the whole thing look less like a boys' club. If you do know me, then you'll know I've earned my place on this sofa a few times over and then some.

The four of us are the show's judges. The giant desks, golden buzzers and uber-glam outfits of future talent show formats are not yet with us. But we are all in our best clobber tonight. The men are in black tie, although Simon has his shirt undone at the neck as usual. I have on a beautiful black dress that's covered in sequins, sleeveless with a high neck. It's from Ben de Lisi and I have to say, I absolutely love it. This series is the first time I've had a stylist picking a wardrobe for me, someone doing my hair and make-up. If you work in television, you either love this kind of thing or you loathe it. I'm fully embracing it. Why not? Until a few weeks ago I was buying my own wardrobe, usually from Warehouse, and putting a bit of lippy on myself before the show. (Such is my devotion to Warehouse in fact, that the head of PR there called me earlier this week, having clocked me wearing their stuff. She wanted to know the name of my stylist so they could send me some more clothes. 'It's me,' I chuckled, 'I'm the stylist.') My hairdresser, Gabriella, also tells me people are coming into the salon asking for a 'Nicki chop', which I find very amusing because I have such difficult hair. As a publicist working with entertainers and artists, I've always excelled at being behind the scenes. Annie Lennox is in the studio audience tonight, with her two daughters. I've been working with Annie for years and I have never felt more content or privileged than when watching her perform from the wings. (She's been teasing me throughout this series, calling me the Devil for putting these youngsters through it. She's here tonight though and that means a lot.) But I am happy to admit that I'm enjoying the spotlight being on me just this little bit (OK, so I'm a tad vain!). This moment isn't going to last for ever, I have a day job that I'm not giving up any time soon, so I'm making the most of it.

It's been a long evening. The show you see on television is only a fraction of what happens in the studio, and the excitement and anticipation has built and built. We've watched all the final performances and seen all the back-story videos, and now it's here. The voting has closed and it is time to find out who has won. We judges genuinely have no idea who it will be, although I did spot Simon Cowell shaking his head at his brother Nicholas who is in the audience, just a few moments ago. I wonder if he knows something I don't. I take a quick glance at my watch, a beautiful gift from Gary Barlow (did you hear that name-drop?). It must be time now.

The stage – brilliantly designed, all chrome and blue lights, like a nightclub – is swathed in dry ice and somewhere in the haze stand Ant McPartlin and his co-presenter Declan Donnelly. Gorgeous Ant and Dec, they really have been the invisible glue of this series. They've held it all together and given us so many laughs, usually at Simon or Pete's expense. They're both still fresh-faced young men, in their mid-twenties, not yet the Saturday-night TV institutions they will become.

Between them stand the two even younger finalists, Will Young and Gareth Gates. I can't call either of them unknowns at this point, although that's exactly what they were only three months ago. They're both doing their best fixed smiles, but I can see the terror in their eyes, and they are both fidgeting around. How to stand, how to hold yourself while waiting for a verdict on live television that will make or break your career is not yet something many singers ever need to even think about. Seemingly in an attempt to increase everyone's agony, Dec says:

'You've both performed brilliantly this evening. And it's been very, very, VERY close. One of you got 4.6 million votes. The other one of you got 4.1 million votes. A total of 8.7 million votes. It's a new British record. Whatever happens, it's going to go in the *Guinness Book of Records* as the biggest TV vote Britain has ever seen.'

Well, that's a bit of news. I hadn't anticipated that when I first started working on this concept. I don't think anyone had. The way people have entered into the spirit of this programme from the start has been quite surprising for all of us involved. What this incredible number of votes says about voter apathy and the state of British politics will be discussed on the *Today* programme, *Channel 4 News* and plenty of other 'serious' media in the coming weeks. It's an astonishing feat, to galvanise all those people, at a time when we have record-low turnouts in general and local elections. It was Simon Fuller's idea to give Gareth and Will their own dedicated 'battle buses' and hit the road to campaign for votes, a strategy that came straight from the electioneering playbook. Only it was all to elect a pop star, not a politician.

But right now, the significance of this event in the context of democracy, the music industry and all the other things this show seems to catalyse is not something I'm considering. My mind is jumping around, thinking about everything that will need to happen after the show, all the calls I'll need to make in the morning. The press and interviews I'll need to book in for them both. We learned a lot of lessons last year with *Popstars* and the winners of that show, the band Hear'Say. The tide of feverish adoration those five talented youngsters left that show on is starting to turn. They've produced the UK's fastest-selling debut number 1 single and put on a sell-out tour this year. But fame is a fickle friend. Their lives have been upended and some of them are really feeling the pressure. Whoever said all press is good press clearly hasn't experienced the *Popstars* phenomenon.

So with *Pop Idol*, Simon Fuller wants the finalists to withdraw, take a little disco nap as it were.

'The nation is full up with Gareth and Will,' he's said. 'They'll tire of them if we're not careful.'

He's right, of course. But as their publicist and part of their management team, that's a tall order for me. I know I will have requests tomorrow from all the television shows, *This Morning* and *Top of the Pops*, *SMTV*, all their local television news programmes. All the papers will want to interview them. The tabloids really are the kingmakers right now, and they will need feeding. I'll have to think very carefully about what we say yes to and what we hold off on. I know I'll be up late tonight, talking it all through with my husband Shacky, who has been in the audience all evening. He'll be working with Will and Gareth over at the record label as well, looking after the international side of things. I wonder what he's going to say about it all.

My focus is brought back to the studio by the silence that falls as Ant says it's time to reveal the winner. The audience is fully hysterical now. Everyone is standing up, as though standing will speed things up. I can feel my heart beating in my throat.

Ant says: 'OK guys.'

Simon whispers at me through his teeth: 'Are we ready for this?' as Ant says: 'The winner of *Pop Idol* 2002 is . . . WILL!'

Now the studio audience, already bubbling up like fizzy pop, goes wild. It is genuinely a surprise to hear that Will has won. I'm happy for him, but because I'll be working with them both at the record label, I'm also immediately feeling for Gareth who, at seventeen, is still so young and I think will probably struggle with the losing more than Will, who is longer in the tooth at twenty-three. Will is beaming at his family in the audience, his twin brother especially, and I feel for him too. He obviously wants to run and hug them all but instead has to go and sing the winner's single, 'Evergreen', for what feels like the twenty-seventh time this evening, while the entire studio is bouncing up and down. We all stand up, I'm glad to be off that little sofa, and try to pretend we are watching him while the chaos rumbles around behind us.

'You're the only girl that I need, cause you're more beautiful than I have ever seen,' sings Will, his wonderful falsetto voice and broad perma grin in full effect.

More and more people are gathering on the stage now. Poor Kate Thornton, the presenter, is there trying to keep the whole thing together, Will's and Gareth's families are all hugging and crying. As the silver ticker tape falls down over them like disco confetti, somewhere somebody shouts 'That's a wrap!' The main lights come on and I feel a huge sense of relief. It's the end not only of a crazy night but a crazy couple of years.

The idea for *Pop Idol* began to germinate back in the late 1990s, before *Popstars* and Hear'Say had been such a success. *Pop Idol* was different though, because for the first time, it would involve public participation. As Simon Fuller's Creative Director at 19 Entertainment, I've been involved in getting the show off the ground from the start: the planning, the early pitches to ITV, and the legal process of creating a show that involves public votes. It's complicated, let me tell you. In many ways, it's an old, tried and tested format, a simple talent show. Not that different to the talent shows of my childhood that I would watch with my parents on Saturday nights, shows like *Opportunity Knocks* and *Stars in Their Eyes*. But now we have telephone voting making it accessible for everyone, not just a studio audience.

In the next few weeks I'll also be going on the road with the show. In fact, I'll be hosting the final night of the tour just over the way at the Wembley Arena. I've never done anything like this before. Simon (Fuller, not Cowell) has pretty much just thrown a microphone at me and with total faith said 'You'll be brilliant!' Me on stage, talking to an audience of 12,000 screaming teenagers and their parents. The first stadium gig I went to was Genesis at the NEC in 1984. I loved it so much, and felt it so hard, that I came home feeling genuinely depressed and worried that I might never experience something like that again.

Now here I am at the *Pop Idol* final, looking at Simon Cowell, whose record label will be signing both Will and Gareth (and the lovely Darius, who didn't make it to the final two but had star written all over him nevertheless). We are both aware of the pressing need to talk to Gareth. He has been the bookies' favourite all week so this will be hard for him, he's still so young. He's stood on the stage with his little sticky-up hairdo and his white suit, looking like an actual angel, trying his hardest to look happy for Will. I signal to him to come down and, with Simon, we go back to his dressing room. Runners with walkie-talkies are whizzing up and down the corridor outside, production people are shouting at each other as they attempt to get everyone out and wrap up the evening. I want to take a moment to reassure this sweet boy that this is just the beginning for him.

The room is full of balloons and flowers and good-luck cards. Simon speaks quietly and in his usual considered way, even though there is so much going on outside and we are all aware that Gareth needs to get back on that stage. Simon looks him straight in the eye: 'OK Gareth, you didn't win the show this evening, but we don't want you to think of this as a loss in any way. You are also a winner tonight and you're going to have a career of your own.'

Giving Gareth a hug, I add: 'Please don't worry, you were so brilliant tonight. You should be really proud of yourself.'

'Thanks, that means a lot,' he says as we leave the room, and I'm glad we've done this as he looks genuinely reassured and slightly less heartbroken. I'm reminded of the responsibility I have; that's why I always say I 'look after' my artists. Because very often that's what this job is.

I walk back with Gareth to the studio. Will, well-mannered and considerate as ever, is beckoning him to come back to the stage and share the moment. I watch them both disappear into the shoal of happy people moving as one on the stage. Now I just want to find Shacky and get home, back to west London. It's been a bit like waiting for exam results tonight and I am relieved to know what I've got at last, but I'm also worn out with it all.

As our car pulls out of the studios, a few of the paparazzi snappers are still there, waiting for their money shots. They'll be up all night, that lot, getting their photos to picture desks and editors all over the country in time for the Sunday papers. They take a few of me and Shacky through the car window and it occurs to me this is probably the last time this sort of thing will happen now the show's over. I think about Mum and Dad as well; I wonder if they enjoyed watching tonight. Funny to think when I left school in Herne Bay all those years ago with my three O levels (always A for effort, C for achievement) I thought maybe I'd be a make-up artist. Now I'm at Wembley getting papped.

As we sweep over the Westway towards home, all of London is twinkling in the night below us. I close my eyes and rest my head on Shacky's shoulder. The *Pop Idol* final is over, but my work has just begun.

2

I Should Be So Lucky

I'm in the Cross Keys pub in Covent Garden, drinking my orange juice and waiting for James Bond to arrive. Not the secret agent, although he is kind of a secret boyfriend and his name really is James Bond, an association he's naturally very pleased about. Apparently, his dad is called James Bond as well, it's a family name. He's a colleague from work I've been seeing, although no one at work knows because we're trying to keep it professional and all that.

James is a salesman at Océ, and I'm the personal assistant to the sales director. Océ is a Dutch firm that manufactures and sells photocopiers to companies all over the world. No one has ever heard of it, so I always tell people it's like Rank Xerox and then they seem to get it. I've done work experience here a couple of times over the years, as my dad, who is also a senior salesman, works here – nothing like a bit of good old nepotism. I'm now here full time, at the company HQ in High Holborn. It's quite a good job. I like my boss Peter, and the pay isn't bad for a twenty-year-old; I'm on £9,500 a year, which I'm pretty chuffed about. Perhaps college was worth it.

But to say it's not my dream job is an understatement. Last year I went to Sydney, Australia, for eight months and stayed with my exotic relatives, Aunty Liz and Uncle Bob, and my cousins Emma and Jon. I say exotic: they just seem exotic because they live so far away in the sunshine and have such a fun attitude to life. They work hard but they play hard too. I loved it there; I had an absolute blast in Sydney. Emma and I both had jobs selling West Coast Coolers, drinks that taste a bit like Babycham, on the market by the beach. Now I'm trying to save enough money to get back as soon as I can. I feel like there's a future there for a girl like me. It doesn't matter what qualifications I have (very few) or whether I passed the 11+ (I didn't). I think I can make something of myself there, something more exciting than working in photocopiers.

But even though in my mind I'm only here in England temporarily, I know I need a different job while I wait for my future to start. I've decided I want to get a job in the music industry. My friend Andrea has inspired me. When we were at college together Andrea did her work experience at CBS (Columbia Broadcasting System) Records in Soho.

She came back from her week there with loads of black and white signed prints of Prefab Sprout, Sade and Wham!, and all these other artists that were signed to CBS who she'd met and been to see live and had blagged backstage passes for. She knows she is going to work in the music industry. She's like me, no degree or A levels, we've both just got our BTEC national diplomas in business studies. But I think she's a bit of a visionary. She just decides to do stuff if she wants to, and doesn't worry about failing. And it has planted a seed in my mind. Why can't I work in the music industry too?

I absolutely love music. I listen to music all the time, all kinds. I'm not a snob about it like some people. Growing up in Herne Bay there's not a lot of live bands to see – not big names anyway. We just go to pubs, mostly. But I saw the Smiths at the Margate Winter Gardens, and Tight Fit. From one side of the music spectrum to another, you might say. There's not much live music I won't watch, apart from some of the heavy rock stuff. But I loved Midnight Oil and INXS when I saw them in Sydney. There is something about being in an audience. The magic of a stage with all the lights and the smoke and seeing the emotion on the band's faces flicks a switch in me.

You could say I grew up on the stage, or at least on the side of it, behind the curtains. My family was big into amateur dramatics when I was little, and Mum worked alongside the local director. I spent whole weekends sitting in the flippy chairs at the King's Hall with my older sister Shelley, watching the auditions. I loved seeing all the wardrobe and make-up at work, the scenery being painted, all the backstage stuff. I didn't particularly want to be the one performing (I know my limits); it was thrilling enough just to be in the wings.

Anyway, if I'm going to go to work every day while I'm here, I might as well do something that excites me. And if Andrea from college can just go out and get a job in the music industry because she's determined and focused enough, why can't I?

I've got a copy of *Ms London* I picked up at Holborn tube this morning – there are always hundreds of copies scattered around by the ticket machines – and I'm looking for jobs while I wait for James Bond. We often come here because it's not far from work, but far enough away that no one we know from work will see us. It's a small, dark, Victorian pub with wood panelling and sticky red carpet, but it's cosy and I feel quite comfortable here on my own. Kathleen Turner is on the front cover of *Ms London* looking ravishing (my perm is meant to look like her hair but somehow doesn't), and there's an article about how to inject romance into your wardrobe. I flick through the pages to the back where the jobs are always listed. Endless secretarial roles at life assurance companies and businesses that are just lists of surnames: Willis, Faber, Thornton, Smith. I move my frosted pink fingernail down the listings, one by one.

Two jobs catch my eye. One is at CBS, which is where

Andrea did her work experience. That would be good, although it is in the legal department and if that is anything like the legal department at Océ it doesn't appeal to me. It would mean endlessly faxing contracts back and forth, and tons of admin. Not my forte. The other is at RCA Records in the sales department, which sounds a bit more like it, although I already work with a team of salesmen, albeit the photocopier variety. It would be good to get a bit closer to the stars and, most importantly, their music. Why work in the music industry otherwise?

'Hello gorgeous,' says James Bond as he strides into the pub in his suit. Double-breasted, of course. He can definitely work a suit. 'How's the job hunt? Found anything in the music biz yet?'

James is a couple of years older than me and has his own flat in Teddington. Since I came back from Sydney, I've been commuting from my parents' house in Herne Bay most of the week, still in my childhood bedroom with my single bed, and my pine dressing table with the triple mirror and the matching stool. Being James's girlfriend is giving me a glimpse of a different life, the life of a young professional in London, and I like it. As with most of the salesmen at work he's got plenty of charisma and charm. It helps that he looks like a tall Tom Cruise and drives a company car (easily impressed, moi?). We usually meet up after work for a drink in the week and he drives me to Victoria Station for my train home. At weekends I stay with him at his flat and we often end up going out with his friends. They're all older than me; some are married already, and have very different jobs. They're teachers and lawyers, some of them work at the BBC, and we go out for long Sunday lunches at pubs on the river with polished wooden floors and big white dining plates – pubs that are not remotely like the old boozers in Herne Bay, or the one we're in now.

'You know what, James, I think I can do a couple of these jobs. I've got the right experience. Do you think I should apply?' I ask, although I'm not really asking for his opinion.

'What harm is there in trying? Go for it!' he says. 'Hold on a minute,' he says as an afterthought. 'I think I know someone who works on *Top of the Pops*.'

'Of course you do.' I'm rolling my eyes, only being half sarcastic. If anyone is going to know someone who works in television it's James.

'One of Leslie's housemates, Mary. I think she's part of the production team, something like that? Let me see if she knows anyone who can help you. Stay there.'

I know Leslie from recent weekends in Richmond. She's brilliant but I'm fairly certain she has better things to do than help me find a job. James goes to the payphone at the far end of the bar and I chuckle to myself as he flicks through his little Filofax to find the number. This is why I like being with him. He's a bit like Andrea – he makes things happen. I spend a lot of time around salesmen, and they are all like that, I think – impatient, but in a good way. He starts talking and sticks his thumb up at me while he's chatting. He comes back all smiles.

'Leslie says Mary says there's a job at MCA, in promotions. They need a secretary. She's going to find out for you.' Simple as that. 'Drink?' he adds as he heads to the bar.

Over the next week or so, Leslie turns out to be a real-life angel. Not only is there a job going at MCA Records (full title, the Music Corporation of America), but she tells her friend I'd be good for the job. Mary phones the guy there, a man called Graham, and she tells him I'm amazing and he should hire me. I've never even met Mary! I am too invested in the thrill of it all right now to properly process the significance of this kindness from a stranger – two strangers, both women. But somewhere in the back of my mind, a note is made that this is something good someone has done for me, and I will always try to pay it forward.

Two weeks later and I am sitting on a bench in Soho Square, staring at the funny little Tudor-looking house in the middle of the square and eating my prawn sandwiches from the sandwich bar (white bread, always white bread) before I go to my third interview of the day. It's the one at MCA, the one I think I want most. It's cold but sunny and fresh, and most of the benches are full with people also eating their sandwiches. I wonder what they all do for a living. Are they my future colleagues? I called in sick at Océ this morning, something I never do and I feel truly awful about. I don't like to lie, it doesn't come naturally to me. I didn't have a choice though. I know that this is the direction I'm meant to be heading in. I've had my interviews at RCA and CBS, over the other side of the Square, and they went well. But they both felt a little too close to the job I've already got. Corporate, if you know what I mean. I'd be one of a number of other typists in an office. MCA feels like something else. I think because it's come through a friend, it feels more real.

I finish my sandwich and stand up to straighten my outfit. I'm wearing my black tube skirt and a top that's very slightly off the shoulder with my denim jacket over it, with my wide, low-slung belt and my brown suede stilettos from Dolcis that I love. It feels odd to be wearing such fashionable clothes to an interview but Leslie says no one wears ordinary smart office clothes at these sorts of places. It's OK to look cool. I hope I look cool. Do I?

Leslie says they want secretarial support in the promotions department. I know enough about how this business works by now to understand that the promotions department in a record company is pretty important. You've got the A&R department, which finds, signs and develops the singers and musicians who make the music; the marketing department that comes up with how their albums look and works out who their fans are and generally sprinkle the magic; the legals, who work out all the contracts; and the sales department, who get the physical records and tapes distributed and sold. It's like a huge jigsaw puzzle made up of so many important parts. You can have a great song and you can have it on sale in all the shops, but if no one sees it being performed on television or hears it on the radio on their way to work, no one will know it exists, and no one is going to buy it. So promotions are essential to the success of a song, and to the financial success of the company. I like the idea of doing something creative, the thought of working with television programmes and radio shows. It sounds less like a job and more like a whole lot of fun to me. My passion for music and a career all rolled into one.

The MCA office is in Brewer Street, a couple of streets back from the more savoury end of Soho and smack bang in the middle of what is still very much a red-light district. As I make my way down the street I step over empty bottles and cardboard boxes that spill out from the bars and clubs onto the pavement. The neon signs for Madame Jojo's are winking at me from down the road as I push the door into the reception area of MCA. I hear someone thundering down the stairs to welcome me.

'Hi, Nicki? I'm Graham, come on up to the office.'

Well. Graham is very good-looking. No one warned me about that, did they? He's better looking than James! He's cool – he's wearing Levi 501s and a tight white T-shirt and cowboy boots, like something from the Levi's advert where the man comes down in his pants and keeps his jeans in the fridge – and oh my goodness he smells amazing. I try not to let my jaw drop too far, and follow him up the narrow stairs. There are boxes of files and piles of vinyl everywhere, and he leads me along a corridor, past a few open doors. It's really noisy in here! I hear a song I know by Transvision Vamp, 'I Want Your Love', blasting out of one door. Graham closes it as we pass, and I can hear the voice of Steve Wright talking on Radio 1 as we pass another. I glimpse a man in a leather jacket talking on the phone. This place is already a different world to the purpose-built offices of my current job. There are no big windows or carpet tiles or typists clacking away. It's a rabbit warren, with something fascinating behind every door. The floor is uneven underfoot and the walls are covered in posters and gold discs in frames. There are tapes, paperwork, records and telephones on every desk. We come to a central room with a few empty desks and huge whiteboards with writing on them. I see artist names: Transvision Vamp, Holly Johnson. Eric B. & Rakim. And in the column next to them the names of television shows I know, *Wogan* and *Des O'Connor Tonight*, *Get Fresh*, *TV-am*.

We sit down at one of the desks. I'm opposite him, trying not to let him know that I have clocked how handsome he is. I suspect he knows only too well how handsome he is anyway. The old sash window is slightly open, propped up by a VHS tape, and the sound of bikes and car horns tooting below in Brewer Street filters in, adding to the sense of urgency I'm feeling. I need to work here.

'So, you've been to Australia?' he asks.

It's funny, the eight months I spent in Australia last year have been a real talking point in every interview I've had.

The Australian pop music scene is huge at the moment. Everyone's gone mad for *Neighbours* and *Home and Away*, a spread called Vegemite, and Kylie Minogue's 'I Should Be So Lucky' was a big number 1 earlier this year. 'Beds Are Burning' by Midnight Oil is still on everywhere you go. The world is obsessed with all things Aussie, and I have actually been there. Perhaps it impresses people? Plus not many girls my age have left home and been so far away by themselves. I like to think this says I'm plucky and adventurous. In truth I am just lucky to have cousins and a family there who I stayed with. I'm still telling myself it's my intention to get back there if I can, but I'm not going to mention any of this to Graham just now. Best not.

'Yes, I fell in love with Sydney. The city, not the boy,' I joke.

We chat about what I do at Océ and what he's looking for. He says the department needs someone to organise them all a bit (those boxes on the stairs), do the admin, send out singles and albums to producers and bookers, book restaurants and taxis, and hold the fort when they're all out. I can do that, Graham. Oh yes indeed.

The pay, he says, is £7,500, a full £2,000 less a year than I am currently earning, but I don't let Graham know I'd be taking a pay cut. I don't want anything to jeopardise my chances. Not for the last time, I clock myself making a big decision about my career that has absolutely nothing to do with earning more money or improving my finances.

Saying my goodbyes to Graham, I close the door behind

me and step back out into the cold Soho street. A woman in a very skimpy outfit is standing in a doorway smoking. Thursday afternoon is becoming Thursday evening and people are starting to filter out of doorways and into the pubs that occupy every corner here. The street is alive with possibility, and again I feel a powerful certainty that this is the job I am meant to have. I know, I just absolutely know. It's nothing to do with the way Graham looks either.

I'm not seeing James tonight so I go to catch my train home and stare forlornly out of the window all the way back to Herne Bay. I'm feeling something close to heartache, like I've just met the love of my life and I'm now in agony waiting for his call. Later on I even dream about the job. I'm walking to work down Brewer Street in my brown stilettos and I stop and talk to that woman in the doorway and she turns into Wendy James from Transvision Vamp and she and I are dancing on the stairs up to the office. I think that's what they call a fait accompli, in my dreams anyway.

The next day at work I am so distracted I cannot think straight at all. My boss Peter asks me if I'm OK and should I have come back to work today if I'm still unwell? For a minute I don't know what he's talking about but then I remember I was meant to be ill yesterday. I excuse myself and go to find an empty office. I pick up the phone and dial 9 for an outside line, hesitate for a second, and then punch in the rest of the numbers that are written on the piece of paper currently shaking in my hand.

Graham answers and I say: 'Hi Graham, it's Nicki Chapman. Graham, I dreamt about your job last night.'

'Oh right?' he answers, confused and probably a little bit scared.

'Yes, I dreamt you gave me the job! And I really, really want to work for you, Graham. The thing is, I've been offered the other two jobs I interviewed for yesterday. But yours is the job I want. So please can you put me out of my misery and tell me whether I've got the job or not, because what I don't want to do is say yes to RCA or CBS, and then you come back and offer it to me.'

Without a second's hesitation, he goes: 'Yeah, all right then, you can have the job. Start as soon as you can.'

On the train home this time I'm beaming to myself and I don't care if anyone thinks I'm bonkers. I can't quite believe I did that. It was out of character for me to call him up like that and get the answer there and then. But it worked, Nicki. Maybe being around all these salesmen has rubbed off on me after all. A part of me wants to believe he was blown away by my chat at the interview and maybe he respects my chutzpah for making that call, but a bigger part of me suspects he said yes because it was the easiest thing to do at the time and it meant he didn't have to think about it any more or interview anyone else. Either way, it doesn't matter. I got the job! I've told Peter and he says he's happy for me. What he actually said was 'You'll fly, Nicki.' It brought a little tear to my eye because I didn't know he thought so highly of me. He was just one of those people: a kind, lovely man.

It takes me almost two hours to get home to Herne Bay every day. Two hours and a crazy early start every morning. The hours are going to be very different now I work in the music industry. Graham has warned me there will be late nights and early starts. I can't wait. Before I get into bed I stand at my window and take in the view I've looked at every single night since I can remember. I can see the sea and the pier stretching out from the beach, all from my bedroom. As I close the window and pull the curtains, the familiar sea air fills my lungs. I'll always love it here. But I know that the time has come for me to leave home, my parents, my sister and the little cul-de-sac where I grew up. London, here I come.

3

Room At The Top

It's Monday morning in Brewer Street and the heads of department are arriving at the office for the 10 a.m. promo meeting. There was an Adam Ant gig at the Electric Ballroom in Camden on Saturday that we all went to. It was amazing; he played all his hits. A few of them carried on afterwards and are looking a bit worse for wear, as they often tend to on a Monday. I think it's what they call an occupational hazard.

There are always a few comedy groans as people reach the top of the stairs. The company is spread over six floors and these Monday meetings are always in the MD's office on, luckily, the first floor. There's a whiff of bacon sandwiches and cigarette smoke.

My boss Graham, Head of Promotions, arrives with Phil

Smith, who is Head of TV. He's clutching his cup of tea in a foam cup. 'Pass the sugar, Nicki,' Phil says brusquely as he finds his spot at the far end of the table. Tony (Tony Powell, or TP) is the Managing Director of MCA Records, but Phil has more of the top dog air about him than Tony and Graham. He might not be tall but he definitely has a presence. I think because he's Head of TV and he knows all the producers and presenters, he's the unofficial gatekeeper to the glittering land of entertainment. Everyone defers to Phil, even if they're not aware they're doing it. I shoot the box of sugar cubes along the desk towards him like I'm sending a bourbon down the bar, on the rocks. 'Morning!'

We have this meeting every Monday. It's how we all know what everyone else is doing. All the heads of department are here: marketing, A&R (that's artists and repertoire, the people who find and sign the new talent), press, sales, legal and then Phil, Graham and me. Graham brings me along because I put together the weekly report for everyone that lists all the shows the department has our artists appearing on. Everyone calls it the Bible, and I write it.

Tony's office is by far the largest room in the building but you wouldn't know that it's the office of the boss of a major record label. Apart from the table we're all gathering around, smoky grey glass with tube-shaped chrome legs, an unusual painting (which happens to be by Holly Johnson), a few photos and Tony's desk by the window, there's not much to suggest anything important happens in here. There's a couple of sorry-looking cheese plants at the end by the window and his expensive-looking leather jacket always hangs on the door. I wonder if anyone in the street below listening to music on their Walkmans has any idea about what is happening up above them.

People are still filing in. Here's Tony in his denim shirt, always the denim shirt, and lovely Liz, his PA. Sometimes I think it's Liz who rules the roost here. She's definitely the most rock'n'roll thing about Tony. No one can get near Tony without having to fight Liz first. I'm sure I heard someone refer to her as the Rottweiler. She has the most amazing legs and always wears short denim skirts with cowboy boots and a pair of black Ray-Bans, all day every day. Let's not worry if it's the middle of winter or raining. I honestly don't know if I've seen her face without those sunglasses. She even types in them. She's got one of those sexy husky voices that certain girls seem to have. Is it the cigarettes that do it? I don't know. Anyway she and Tony seem to have a great relationship; she bosses him around, but in a funny, friendly way. Tells him he's not allowed to do this or that, reminds him to eat something. He loves it and often winks at me when she does it, as if to say *there she goes again*. I've never seen him be suggestive or leery or anything like that with her. It's the first time I've seen that kind of mutual relationship between a boss and his PA, or a man and a woman. It's like a friendship, I suppose, and I have to say I admire it. And to be fair Liz is always lovely to me. She always asks how I am and if I'm OK, always lets me see Tony if I need to ask him something. There aren't many other women in that position in the building, so I'm extra glad she's nice to me.

Everyone's here now so the meeting begins with the all-important chart positions for our artists, which were released on Sunday afternoon. Not that long ago I was religiously taping the Top 40 on Sundays from my bedroom and now I'm here with people talking about it in forensic detail at the place where I work. Then we go through the MCA artists currently releasing either singles or albums, and all the heads of department tell everyone else what's happening in their corner. Who's releasing new material, what mixes have been cut, who's going on tour, new signings, possible opportunities. Are we going to have a hit any time soon and who is it going to be? That's basically the big question underneath all the other questions. Eventually we always get to the bit where Tony asks:

'Where are we with promotion?'

I distribute the Bible to everyone. I've put it together with plastic side binders so it looks really smart. It contains all the information about the television and radio shows our artists are appearing and performing on. All those in the meeting seem to be interested in promotions, I guess because ultimately it's the thing that makes or breaks their act. It's also something they have an opinion about. Everyone watches television and listens to the radio, so that makes every single person in this room an expert. Or so they think.

Phil talks through it. Transvision Vamp are on *Going Live!* next week. Holly Johnson's new album, *Blast*, is out soon, there's a lot of anticipation about his solo career after leaving Frankie Goes to Hollywood, he's going on *Top of the Pops* with 'Love Train'. We've signed a new US hip-hop act, Eric B. & Rakim, to look after. They're massive in America but we haven't got much airplay here yet for their album *Follow the Leader*. Phil goes on through the list of artists: Tiffany, Kim Wilde, Jody Watley.

I'm still only the assistant to the department, so I don't say anything much in these meetings. Although people ask me stuff all the time. Is that right, Nicki? Can you check, Nicki? Can you call them, Nicki? I've only been here six months but I'm feeling increasingly useful. And I'm watching it all. I've learned that in some ways promotions isn't too different from sales: it's about making sure the presenters and producers of the television shows that have music on, know all about your artist and when their new song or album is coming out. It's about really plugging away at them to get your artists' songs played so that people go out and buy their records. (That's why people in promotions are called pluggers.) Getting the right exposure over every other record company's acts. Like in sales, you have to be passionate about your product to be any good at selling it. I'm not doing any of that yet and I haven't met many women taking on that role, apart from Andi Taylor, who does Radio 1, and is damn good at it. It's all slightly older men, like Graham and Phil. But I'm starting to feel more and more like I could do it. Mostly though I still can't believe I'm working here at all. I can't believe this is a job – my job. To think I could still be typing up photocopying contracts over in Holborn.

The Bible also tells everyone about the plays we've had on the radio, mostly Radio 1, Capital Radio and Radio 2 along with the independent local stations. Graham, still as handsome as when he hired me a few months ago, talks everyone through the radio stats. The guys in the sales team always find this useful to know because they can sell more records to the shops if a song is getting a lot of airplay. All the big music retailers like Tower, Our Price and HMV are likelier to take our records if everyone's heard Bruno Brookes, Gary Davies or Steve Wright playing them on Radio 1. But video has definitely killed the radio star a little bit, and television is becoming a huge focus for promotion. New television shows are coming on all the time, especially for the kids. There's *Going Live!,* The Box channel on cable TV, and a new show called *The O-Zone* coming soon. They're all opportunities for us to showcase artists and, unlike radio, you get to see the band as well as hear them. It really helps to sell more records, plain and simple.

Graham wraps up and I notice people are getting fidgety. The meeting has run on too long and they all want to get out of here now. Filofaxes are slapped shut and the office is empty in a matter of moments. I clear away the rubbish and head next door to get back to my desk to start typing.

I type all day. I type letters, press releases, labels for samples. I type on an electric typewriter, like the one I learned on at college, carriage return and all that. But Graham says we might be getting a word processor soon, whatever that is. My typewriter is perfectly efficient, I don't think it would be humanly possible to do my job any faster than I already do.

When I'm not typing away I'm usually duping up the videos. The promotions department sends VHS tapes out to all the producers of the television shows. That's how they know if they want our artists on the show or not. I have to get the master copy of the video, which is usually on a U-matic, kind of like a giant audio cassette. I put it into the duping machine in the cupboard that has eight VCR machines underneath it and I hit Record and it records from the U-matic onto all those videos at the same time. It's magic. We have a company that does this for us too, but if I need a dupe quickly I'll go and do it myself. Also it gives me an excuse to watch music videos again and again. Then I type up the labels for the dupes, stick them on and have them biked to wherever they need to go.

I send bikes all over London like you wouldn't believe. Eight, maybe ten motorbike couriers a day. Every time I sit down to do something Phil or Graham shouts 'Nicki, can you bike a video over to Radio 1?' I have a huge purchase order pad and I rip through it and no one ever seems to worry about how much it costs. Don't ask me where the money comes from. It wasn't like that at Océ. The couriers come into reception in their leathers and helmets and I run down to them with the parcels. I send vinyl too, and CDs, to radio stations, although really they need to be taken by hand and delivered to the producers' pigeonholes. Then they can pick them up and listen to them later. It's a short walk to Egton House, where Radio 1 is based, so from here it should be easy to do. But when you're up two or three flights of stairs it's more of a faff than just sending a VHS on a bike, so most of the guys in promotions don't bother as much with sending samples to radio. Not as much as they should.

Mondays are always a long day. I leave work at 7 p.m. and start my journey home. It's a good job I live in London now! One of James Bond's friends had a room going in a house right on the river in Putney, so I took it. £100 a month, plus bills. Not too bad. I didn't know anyone living there or in Putney at all but I didn't want to move in with James – not that we even talked about it, it was just kind of accepted that living together wasn't happening. I'm not sure how long we'll be together, if I'm honest. It's an old house with high ceilings and big windows, three storeys high, Victorian I think. I'm on the top floor. It's only a small single room, and there's a bucket on the stairs that catches the water where the roof leaks when it rains. I don't mind though, it's a fab house. All the decor is a bit old-fashioned but in a cool way;

the furniture looks like it belonged to someone's zany bohemian grandmother. I feel very at home living here.

There are seven other housemates – Gill, Kate, Priscilla, Simon, Conor, Ian and sometimes his brother, Trevor – and they are all mad keen rowers. Imagine that! They all get up at 5 a.m. and go rowing on the Thames before they go to work. Kate and Gill are actually in training for the Commonwealth Games and the Olympics. So when I get up at 7 a.m. every day there's no one at home, they're rowing. Quite often I come home and there's no one home either – they're all rowing, or down at the rowing club. They're lovely, kind, extremely sporty people. No one ever seems to do any housework, and the washing machine is full the whole time with their dirty kit. My mum can't believe it. But there's a proper payphone in the hall so it's easy to call home and talk to Shelley and Mum. I miss them, and Dad, and home quite a bit, especially at the weekends. I hardly notice the days passing in the week but at the weekends I sometimes feel a bit lonely because I don't really know anyone except for the rowers and the people I work with. Last night I spoke to Mum and she said I should come home for the weekend.

'Why don't you come back to Herne Bay if you are feeling fed up? Shelley and I are here, we can go shopping in Canterbury.'

'No Mum, I've got to stick it out. I've got to make proper friends. I can't just be friends with James's friends. I've got to make my own friends.'

Besides, I know that being lonely at weekends is only a temporary thing. It's more than made up for by the thrill of my working week. I've met a couple of famous people at work now as well, and I'm getting used to it being normal. Can I really say that? I'm slightly cringing at the thought of it, but that's the truth. The first star I met properly was Wendy James from Transvision Vamp, my absolute heroine after Debbie Harry. Although she's roughly the same age as me we are worlds apart. She was everything I expected her to be. She came up into the office looking like a doll, peroxide blonde hair, fake tan, wearing this teeny-tiny pink tube dress and big black punky boots with spikes on. She walked straight to Phil's desk and sat on his lap. I don't know what she said to him but he roared with laughter and practically threw her off him. It must have been something saucy. She has so much front in real life, it's easy to see how she fronts a whole band, even though she's so little. She shouted 'Bye Nicki!' at me when she left. I couldn't be more starry-eyed about her. Girl-crush time.

Lying in my little bed tonight, above the rowers who are all fast asleep, I find this morning's promo meeting keeps looping around in my mind. No one is doing anything about Radio 2. It's not exactly the coolest radio station – my mum and dad still listen to Radio 2 because it's got all the 50s, 60s and 70s hits on it. But I've heard Frances Line, the Head of Music there, is trying to do something different. They're losing listeners and need to appeal to a younger audience.

I bet they'd like some stuff, and we've got Lyle Lovett the American country singer, Steve Earle and Nanci Griffith; they'd fit on Radio 2. There's no way Graham or Phil will let me have a go at any of the television shows, Phil guards them too fiercely, but I reckon if I suggest I do Radio 2, they'd just be grateful I'm offering. It won't affect what I'm already doing, and I can walk over there easily from the office in my lunchtime.

I'll suggest it to Graham in the morning.

4

I Don't Want Your Money, Honey

'I'm not paying you any more money,' Graham says, like he's my dad and I've just asked for a rise in my allowance. I feel myself wince slightly.

The truth is I would probably pay him if he'd let me do it. My capacity for underestimating my worth in this office still seems to know no bounds. It's a good job my rent is so cheap and I don't have an expensive social life.

'I know, I'm not asking for more money. I just really want to do it. Please?' I pretend to pray and do my best fluttery-eyed smile at him.

'Fine,' he says, bemused at my breathless enthusiasm for the least sexy wavelength out there, 'Radio 2 is all yours.'

I skip out of his office and head straight to the pile of samples I've already stacked on my desk, ready to take to

Broadcasting House. I've got Kim Wilde on vinyl, as well as a couple of CDs and an extra-special 'disappearing' CD (coded so that the music only plays six times before it vanishes) with a new track by Lyle Lovett. I've also put a few VHS tapes into the mix for good measure, in case they want to see the video, and I've raided the cupboard for some promo items. I've got a couple of Tiffany T-shirts and a Blue Mercedes Zippo lighter. The studios and offices are just up the road in Regent Street so I'll walk over with them in a backpack. I'm going to get some of our amazing artists on Radio 2, just see if I don't.

Lunchtime comes around, and after I've picked up everyone's sandwiches from the sandwich bar and scoffed mine on the way back to the office (still prawn on white bread) I set off to deliver my records. I've brought my black Reebok high-tops into work today, especially for the walk, and I am certain that I am in fact Melanie Griffith in *Working Girl* as I set out across Soho on my pilgrimage to Radio 2.

I've got a list of all the producers I want to hit; I know all their names from doing the Bible every week. I introduce myself to the girl on reception and she points me to the pigeonholes where I'm to leave all the samples. I pass a few other pluggers – I think sometimes they just wait around hoping to catch the producer or the presenter they want to talk to. I place my samples in, one by one, hoping the neatly typed labels and crisp white sleeves will help them stand out from the others.

I've picked up from overhearing conversations in the office that MCA isn't having the best time. We don't have any real superstars, although there is talk about Nirvana and Guns N' Roses coming on board soon, with a new US rock label called Geffen. But right now, we don't have any massive artists on the roster to plug. In many ways that suits me. I'm not wedded to a genre or a certain band or a look (although I do now own a pair of cowboy boots. It had to be done! £125 from R.Soles on the King's Road. They do wonders for my chunky legs, especially with my little red mini-skirt and my leather jacket). I think because I love live performances I'm open to anything. Lots of people who come into the office seem to be the kind of folk who know every song on every album ever created by their favourite artists, can quote B-sides and dates and all sorts, but have no idea about other genres. I respect that kind of dedication and knowledge, but if you're in promotions, what's the use in being fanatical about Lyle Lovett and country music when your job is to plug a man called Bobby Brown and a whole new genre called new jack swing?

Speaking of Lyle Lovett, I know he and Nanci Griffith are coming over to London next month – they're both American country artists. I leave a little note with the disappearing CD for Frances to ask if any of her presenters would like to interview them. I've spoken to her on the phone a few times when she's called for Graham. It's worth a shot.

Later on, my phone lights up. It is Frances Line calling

to speak to me – actually to me and not Graham or Phil or anyone else. She says thank you for the samples and yes please, she'd like to set up an interview on one of the shows and when would be a good time for Lyle?

Putting the phone down, I can't help letting out a little squeal, like I've just been told I've won a competition or something. I have just got my first airplay on national radio for one of our major American artists.

I rush in to tell Graham, who I think is genuinely pleased and surprised but also can't help laughing at me a little bit. Because it's Radio 2 and not exactly *Top of the Pops*.

I know Radio 2 isn't seen as cool. It's not like Radio 1. If you can get your act on the Radio 1 playlist, you can basically book your holiday to Barbados straight away. Your job is done. Hit made. Once a song is on the playlist, you might get thirty spins a week for that track and your record is going to sell. Your artists will probably get to play on *Top of the Pops* plus all the other television promo you can book. Lyle Lovett on Radio 2 isn't going to be funding anyone's holidays. But it's a start. I feel a sense of pride welling inside me. I want to phone Shelley and tell her, or Mum or Dad, anyone. But I'm also a little bit reluctant to allow that pride to be real. I'm still struggling to believe someone is letting me do this and is paying me for it as well. I would genuinely do this as a hobby.

Why is that? Is it because I'm not particularly well-educated? It has never come up in the office, no one has ever even asked if I went to school or did A levels or university.

They're more interested in the fact I went to Australia. Maybe it's because I'm still young, I'm only twenty-two. The 'plugger' girls I meet from other record labels are confident, sassy women who can really look after themselves. I love fashion and music, all my money goes at Warehouse and Miss Selfridge, but I don't think of myself as edgy like some of them are.

And then there's Graham and Phil, both witty and larger than life and well-connected. There are a lot of very strong personalities and impressive people around the place. I know I can hold my own, outwardly at least. It's just that occasionally I catch myself feeling a bit terrified, like someone is going to find me out and realise that I'm not meant to be here. But all I want is to work in the music industry.

I won't let it hold me back – in fact, in a strange way it makes me need to go further, do better. Maybe I need to prove to myself I deserve to be here. A few of us watched the Brit Awards on television from the office. I hadn't been invited of course, I am still too much of a minion to go to something like that, but Graham and Tony went. It was a total car crash, so much so that people are still laughing about it. I've honestly never seen anything on television so cringey. For some strange reason they had Sam Fox the Page Three model presenting it, with Mick Fleetwood from Fleetwood Mac. He's really tall and she's really short, so they looked ever so funny before it had even started. It was live and the teleprompter kept malfunctioning so they didn't know what they were meant to be saying, and everyone in the audience was getting very drunk and heckling. It felt like it had all been put together with Sellotape. It was meant to be a showcase of the pinnacle of British music. Instead it looked like a sixth-form production. All of us in the office were crawling under the desk with embarrassment, watching the show, but laughing our heads off at the same time. When I got home the guys at the house all teased me, going 'Is this really what you do?'

That evening Annie Lennox won Best British Female Artist. She was so confident and radiant when she accepted her award from Tina Turner. I adore Annie Lennox, she has everything I think a true artist should have. She's authentic and such a talented songwriter. Amazing voice, so much presence. She and Dave Stewart are the real deal and I love the Eurythmics as well. Just a few years ago I used to walk down to the music shop in Herne Bay at the weekends because they listed the singles charts in the window and I would always look to see where the Eurythmics were. I wish there were more women like her in music, more female-fronted bands. Watching her get up on that stage confirmed for me that this is the world I want to work in. I want to be the one organising interviews for the artists, watching them perform, being responsible for their promotion. But this job isn't just about getting their music heard and played on the radio. I want to get into plugging on the TV side of things. That's my new mission.

To get into television I have to get past Phil. Or at least get Phil on side. Or get on Phil's side. One of those. Phil is a tough old nut to crack. He's very funny, always telling jokes or roaring loudly on the phone to someone he's known for years. I do like Phil, but he upset me recently. We actually had a bit of a spat, can you believe? He was on the phone to someone at *Rapido*, the television show with Antoine de Caunes, with the door open and I overheard him blaming me for something he hadn't done. He said: 'Oh bloody hell, it's Nicki. She's useless, sorry. I told her to bike it over and she didn't.'

I was horrified. Not that I had forgotten to do something – I knew I hadn't, I don't forget to do things the boss asks me to do – but that he was talking about me like that to someone in the business. He put the phone down and before I could stop myself I said: 'Phil, you can't say that about me.'

He scoffed a bit. I think he was surprised I'd gone there at all – and said: 'What?'

I repeated: 'You can't say that about me. That's my reputation you're trashing. If I haven't done something, that's fine. But that just wasn't true, what you just said.'

He looked at me agog. His feet were up on the table and he struggled slightly to get them down, and then he muttered some bad joke about how I was just in a strop because I'd split up with James recently.

I don't know where I got the courage from, but that line flicked a switch. I shouted right back at him:

43

'What's that got to do with it? You can't say stuff like that to me!'

He kept smirking and before I could think any better of it I said:

'Why don't you just fuck off, Phil.' I managed to storm out just before he could see that I was crying.

At home later on I sat at the kitchen table with Priscilla. It was unusual to have anyone home and I was grateful for the company. I told her everything and she was really comforting and sweet, told me not to take it personally. Drying my eyes, I asked how her day had been and she casually said someone had had a heart attack on the Tube station floor and that she'd given them mouth-to-mouth (she's a medical student) and then they'd been sick all over her. And that they had later died in the hospital.

Talk about putting things into perspective! No one had died on me today. But I did still tell my boss to eff off. Oh god. What were you thinking, Nicki?

A few days later and Phil still hasn't apologised, but something has changed: he's been asking me to help him out a bit more. He can be very abrupt, as I learned the hard way. I think maybe he knows this about himself. He's not being sheepish, I don't think he's capable of that, but I do think I detect an element of regret in his manner.

Phil knows he can rub people up the wrong way, he's just that kind of man and it's just his style. And I can't forget, he's very successful. I hear him on the phone being bullish: 'Why aren't you playing my act? Why aren't you booking my act?' It's not the way I do things at all. Everyone has their own style, but I'm more … friendly I guess. It's a different way of working, so he's started asking me to make some of his calls for him.

'They're not taking my call, Nicki, give them a call will you?' 'Do us a favour Nicki, ring up *The Chart Show* and find out when they're going to play Kim.'

He calls me the mole because my hearing's not great sometimes and I wear my glasses for typing. He barks orders at me from the other room and I'm like: 'What? Huh?' He screams at me, 'Ring him up for fuck's sake!!' and I have to ask for the number. 'Sorry Phil, I only got the last three digits.' He says it's like working with a fucking mole. But it's all kind of funny and I know he likes it when I laugh at his teasing. And he does love to tease me.

Working for Phil is tough, I'm not going to lie, but he's teaching me the job, getting me in on his calls and deals. I'm grateful for that. He trusts me and he knows I'm keen and trying to learn the ropes from him. I don't regret holding my ground but I do respect him. We are chalk and cheese, but it works. And I'm learning that I can also be quite tolerant, take a step back and see the bigger picture, especially if it means I get more responsibility and closer to the television side.

He's also taking me to Wembley soon to watch Kim Wilde, who is supporting Michael Jackson on his huge global Bad tour. He doesn't have to do that. He says I probably won't get to meet Jacko but I don't mind. I've always been a huge fan of Kim's. 'Kids in America' was the anthem of my youth, and Phil knows how much I worship her. I think underneath his rough exterior, Phil wants to help me, wants to see me realise my dream to be a publicist.

A few months later and when I come into the office after lunch one day, I'm told there's been a terrorist attack on an aeroplane; it's exploded over a town called Lockerbie in Scotland. All 259 people on board have been killed and the plane has scattered into pieces over this tiny Scottish community. Andi, who looks after Radio 1 and Capital, tells me that everyone's shaken because Holly Johnson and his manager Wolfgang were booked on the flight – they were meant to be travelling to New York from London. Someone from the press office across the corridor has assured us all that they're both OK, thankfully they missed the flight because they were stuck in traffic on the way to Heathrow. But the shock and horror about what has happened is no less potent and everyone is watching the television in disbelief at what they are seeing. There's a rumour another musician, Paul Jeffreys, the guitarist from Cockney Rebel, was on the flight as well. A lot of international artists fly that route. The phones are red hot all afternoon with reporters and fans asking if Holly Johnson has died. I don't even know how they know he was meant to be on board or why they are chasing such awful news.

5

Every Little Step I Take

Zoe bundles herself into the car, a gorgeous blast of Diorissimo and fun. 'Morning Chappers!' She bangs a cassette into the stereo and turns up the volume. It's a new dance remix she's got of Bobby Brown's 'My Prerogative'. We are both dancing in our seats and singing 'I can do what I wanna do' as loud as we can as we drive into work.

This car-clubbing session with Zoe has become a bit of a ritual on these morning journeys. She works in the dance music department at MCA, sending all the new remixes out to the clubs and the DJs, Tim Westwood and Pete Tong and all those guys. She's another stunner, tall with a thick mane of blonde hair, and she has a wonderful confidence that I don't feel I have found yet. She left home when she was sixteen and lives with her boyfriend. I love hanging out with her because she's brilliant fun, doesn't take things too seriously and bigs me up all the time. If I say I'm worried about a meeting with someone or an artist I'm working with, she goes 'Oh, balls to them! You're amazing! Don't worry about it!' or something like that. She's just a big breath of fresh air and someone I'm really beginning to think of as a friend here in London. I pick her up most days as she lives nearby and we drive into work together in my, ahem, company car.

Yes, now I'm officially the Television Assistant at MCA I've got a company car. It's a navy blue Peugeot 205 and we are in a deeply committed relationship, this car and me. I've always loved driving and now I find any excuse I can to drive my little Peugeot, complete with a removable stereo cassette player that I carry around with me like a handbag, all over London. I even have my own parking space in the grotty NCP in Brewer Street. Somebody told me that it costs the company about three grand to rent it out for me, though I can't believe that's true.

I also have my own mobile phone. My parents can't believe it. It's a Nokia 101 and I take it everywhere with me, and the charger. I thought I would feel weird or embarrassed about using it but it's actually very handy, especially when I'm with my artists on set or somewhere. I can chase them if they're running late, book a taxi or get a takeaway delivered to a studio so much more easily now.

It's been a thrilling couple of years to say the least. Because

I've been working so closely with Phil and he's been getting me in on his deals, I've started to make a name for myself outside MCA. I'm one of the youngest pluggers in the business, I'm ambitious and I'm a woman, so I'm quite different from some of the others out there. I guess I've started to stand out. I even got properly headhunted by Chrysalis, over in Kensington. I accepted the offer and signed contracts and everything; it was more money and they have some great artists – Sinead O'Connor, among others. But I changed my mind at the last minute. Not great, I know, but it just didn't feel right. It made me realise how much I like MCA and the people here. I've even developed a soft spot for Phil! I've been here a couple of years and there are things I'm not happy about, for sure. But I'm not quite ready to jump yet.

So here I am on my way in to the office. I'm wearing my new black Jigsaw trouser suit, with a blue shirt underneath and my black Chelsea boots. I need to look smart today because I've got a lunch with Phil and then I'm meeting one of my artists. Lunch is at the Japanese restaurant in Brewer Street a couple of doors away from the office. It's my favourite. Can you believe I hadn't ever even tasted Japanese food before a few months ago and now I'm eating sushi and teriyaki three times a week. I love it. Phil and I have pretty much all our meetings there, or if not we do them at Topo Gigio, the Italian in Brewer Street. Everything there is delicious – huge portions and always a giant mountain of Parmesan – and the bill always seems to go on the company credit card. Everyone at work loves it in there. Barely a day goes by that there isn't a crowd from the office still there at 5 p.m., bottle of Chianti number four just being poured. No one seems to mind. I'm not one for those long lunches though, I always feel like I have too much to do. It suits me when they're all down in Topo's, it's quieter for my phone calls. And it suits them to know I'm holding the fort.

Sometimes I worry I'm not like the rest of them. The other day, one of them cracked a joke and I didn't laugh. They turned around and said: 'What's wrong with you?' I said: 'Nothing. It just wasn't very funny.' And he said, straight-faced: 'You're never going to make it in this world, Nicki. You're never, ever going to make it.' I found that quite upsetting. I don't mind if people don't like me or even if they behave badly sometimes, but I don't know why anyone has to be nasty like that. Zoe says it's because I'm a young woman and I'm doing well, he thinks I'm a threat to his career. How ridiculous is that?

I'm pretty good at not reacting to everything these days. I focus on doing my best. Mum and Dad's mantra was always 'Just do your best, Nicki.' And I am. I know I am bringing in sales and that is what I am being paid to do. Like with Adamski, that's who I'm meeting later. His name is Adam but he's called himself Adamski after a man who spotted UFOs or aliens or something. He's the first artist I've been given to look after entirely by myself, not someone I've inherited from Phil. Phil's given him entirely to me; he saw an opportunity and let me run with it. Adam is a brilliant young producer and DJ who has come up through the rave scene. He has beautiful delicate features and platinum blonde hair and a really lovely, kooky way about him. He is passionate about electronic dance music. An incredible wave of new technology is coming in and he's emerging as the face of it. People drive for hours to see him play at raves – it's all aceeed! and Lucozade for energy and they have to call a number on a flyer in a grubby phone box to find out where the latest rave location is. They hardly drink, these ravers, but they often take a serious amount of drugs and dance the night away, thousands of them in a field, having the best time as the sun rises. It's quite an impressive sight. The raves are often held somewhere just off the M25. It's not my scene but I know loads of my friends drive to these open live gigs at the weekends.

Adam's only a year younger than me but I feel more like a mum or a big sister towards him. I think that's why it really works having me do his publicity, because let me tell you he likes to party quite hard. If I did that too we'd never get anything done.

I got him onto a show recently called *The Hit Man and Her*. It's a cult dance music programme on ITV presented by Michaela Strachan and Pete Waterman (who also happens to be the exec producer). Adamski was there to perform his single 'Killer' with a singer called Seal doing the lead vocal. It was filmed at a club in Derby, the Pink Coconut, and as usual Adam made me smuggle his dog in. His dog, Diss, is so cute, a little white Jack Russell. Adam takes him everywhere but I had to hide him in my bag because they don't allow dogs on set. I figured it would be fine. They weren't going on until 2 a.m. so we had a couple of hours to kill before the set started. I left Adam, his mates and Diss the dog while I went and talked to the production people. When I came back Adam had written DISS on his forehead in permanent marker. It was too late to do anything about it so Adam went out and played the whole set with DISS written on his face. I had to calm the producers down as they weren't expecting that; it wasn't part of the set we'd discussed and everyone was in a tizz about whether it was OK. Also, was he OK? It looked a bit cracked, to say the least. What do you do when your artist writes DISS on their head backwards? I'd only left him for half an hour. Thankfully it wasn't a swear word, otherwise the people at ITV would have had a fit. I think he's hilarious, a talented young rave anarchist, and I adore him.

When I speak to Shelley at the weekend, she's really surprised to hear I've gone up to Derby with Adam.

'I'm here working in recruitment and you're off to the Pink Coconut with Adamski and his dog!' she chuckles. 'I've been there a few times for my Northern Soul nights out. Not quite the same!'

There's a lot of nuts and bolts in this plugging job that people don't see. You give the artist or band an opportunity to perform on television but that's just the beginning. Then you have to go and 'cover' the actual show. Covering means you go to the studio with them to make sure everything goes smoothly. I talk to the production team about the sets, organise the equipment and backline (the singers and the dancers behind the main performer), and give everyone a breakdown of the lyrics so they can script the performance correctly with the cameras. I plan the staging, think about what the artist is going to be wearing, book stylists if they are needed, make-up artists, security. I do all of that. Then on the day of filming I make sure the artist knows where they're going, walk around the set with them, and maybe introduce them to the booker and other production staff.

Adam is quite simple to look after. He knows what he wants to look like and only ever has a couple of people in his backline. Some acts, like Bobby Brown for example, have a huge amount of kit, wardrobe and a whole posse of dancers and backing singers to think about. I found myself ironing all his group's trousers recently. But it doesn't faze me, I enjoy all that side of it. Being a child of the am-dram scene definitely has its uses, even if it's not quite on the same level.

Bobby Brown really lived up to his reputation on that recent trip, you know. He came with a huge entourage, eight of them, including his brother and father, all dressed like him and staying by his side wherever he went. He is turning into a massive R&B star and his ego is starting to match. Our Artist Liaison Manager, a guy called Martin Fredrick ('Freddo' to his pals) went to pick Bobby up from the airport in a stretch gold Rolls-Royce. Artist Liaison is the person who looks after the international artists, books their hotels, gets them everything they want. Oils the wheels, shall we say. And Freddo is damn good at it, the best in the business. Don't ask me what happened but apparently the Rolls was all he could get hold of, at vast expense, of course. Bobby was delighted, as you can imagine. Bobby had a record-shop signing in Oxford Street and managed to bring the traffic to a standstill. Thousands of fans turned up, and in the end the police had to remove him from the shop in the back of a van for his own safety and everyone else's. Freddo had to drive the Rolls back to Bobby's hotel in Mayfair – not a problem for him, who has seen it all before and got several T-shirts.

We knew Bobby was going to be in demand while he was here. I confirmed a slot for him on *Wogan* on BBC1 on the Monday night show and he blew everyone away. It was a great performance and a big success. There was a suggestion that he might do an interview with Terry as well but I steered him away from that. Bobby's a great performer, but not such a great talker. I don't think it would have done him any favours. Not that I am inclined to do him any favours ever again after what happened next.

Our next TV opportunity to promote the single was *Top of the Pops* on the Thursday night, which is obviously a big deal for any artist. It was being filmed live – they do that occasionally, though not often – and it was just my luck that this Thursday's show was live. I was with Bobby in the studios in Shepherds Bush in west London, with his dancers and his whole backline. Everyone was there and we'd been rehearsing all day. Around 4 p.m. we were told he was going to take a break. One of his pals came up to me and said, 'Bobby's going to the Hard Rock Cafe, he wants a burger.' He knew full well we were going live on TV at 7 p.m.

I replied: 'Well, I can go and get him a burger.' Ever polite and helpful, Chappers.

The pal said: 'No, no, he wants to go and get one.'

I stood there thinking, *what do I say to this?* I've got no choice really but to let him go and get his burger. He's a grown man, he has his own stretch Rolls-Royce and a driver. I tried to reason to myself that it should only take him thirty minutes or so to get to the Hard Rock at Hyde Park. We'd rehearsed once in the morning, we'd also done the dress rehearsal. Everyone knew what they were doing, so it wasn't the end of the world.

'Fine. But for God's sake, you have to be back by 6 p.m.,' I said as they left.

Six o'clock came around and of course no one had returned. I was starting to panic a bit, so I called his brother Tommy and asked where Bobby was. Tommy picked up the phone and said, monotone:

'Bobby is having a burger.'

I replied: 'Yeah, I know he's having a burger' (and under my breath 'That's what you have at the Hard Rock Cafe. You don't have to be Einstein to work that one out.')

Tommy said: 'Yeah, but he's still eating it.'

'Well, you don't have long, because you're on air soon and it's a LIVE show. Remember?'

'No, you don't understand, Bobby's having a burger. He's not coming back. He's eating his burger and he doesn't want to be disturbed.'

By this point I was speaking so closely into my brick-sized mobile phone that I was practically inside it: 'I don't think you understand. This is *Top of the Pops*. Top. Of. The. Pops. This is the biggest music show we have here.'

The line went dead. I tried him again but he didn't answer. I briefly considered driving over to the Hard Rock Cafe and dragging Bobby Brown out by his baggy trousers. I was kicking myself for letting them all go out at all. I mean, the signs were there he wasn't exactly honourable. Earlier in the week I'd been given an envelope of cash by another member of his team, and been told to find Bobby some 'entertainment'. (I didn't find him any 'entertainment' or keep the cash. I gave it to Tony Powell to deal with. Totally above my pay grade.) So maybe I shouldn't have let them go. I just assumed they'd be responsible. I had to go and explain to the producers of *Top of the Pops* that Bobby Brown wasn't coming back but not because of sex, not drugs, not rock'n'roll. No, he was having a burger. Yep. Seriously. There would a big, Bobby Brown-shaped hole in the live show tonight and it would be all my fault.

Top of the Pops has blacklisted me now. I got an absolute bollocking from the producer, Paul Ciani, he told me they'd never seen anything so unprofessional in all their years. Next time I want one of my artists on there I'm really going to have to fight for it, I know that much. It's been a useful exercise though, in that I won't ever assume artists always want to do the right thing, or care about their own promotion as much as I do. It has made me feel a little bit naive but I've learned a good lesson. Just where is a man's head at, that he feels he can do that? Rehearse all day with all of those people and then just not bother to turn up for the sake of a burger? I mean. Such a gifted artist, but on a totally different planet. He later disappeared with the driver and his entourage in the Rolls-Royce, they all went to a party in Cornwall and cost the record company a small fortune in fees. Surprisingly I wasn't invited. Nor was Freddo, but fortunately he has very big budgets.

Apart from being blacklisted by the most important television show in the country, I'm doing OK I think. As well as the car I've had a small pay rise. I'm on £12,000 a year now. With my first new pay cheque I went out and bought my first proper posh handbag. It's by the designer Mulberry, from their shop in New Bond Street. It's dark blue with a brown trim, and it ties together at the top with a leather rope, like a little sack. I showed it to Priscilla and Gill at home and they both laughed when I told them how much it cost and said it's not even proper leather. Apparently it's made of something called cross-grain and that's not as good as normal leather. I don't care, I love it. Zoe laughed at me as well because in Topo Gigio the other day I put a napkin down on the floor to put the bag on it.

6

I Can See Clearly Now

Something unpleasant happened last night that I'm still trying to process. I've always considered myself to be quite switched on when it comes to men, thought I could always read the signs. I'm not a flirt or a prick-tease, I really know that about myself. I'm seeing Greg, a guy from the sales department at MCA, at the moment and I'm really happy with him, so there's no way I'd be going around flirting anyway. So what happened is puzzling me, because I can't work out why it did.

I thought this chap and I were friends at work and it turns out we're not. The reason I thought we were mates is that we've been having a really good laugh in the office recently. Everyone knows he's a bit of a chancer, I guess that says it all really, but I thought he was funny and we were just two colleagues getting on. He invited me round to his house for dinner yesterday and I thought I'd go because I don't like cooking but I do like dinner, and why not? It's a pleasant thing to do with a friend. Someone I thought was a friend. He knows I'm seeing Greg, and last time I checked it is OK to get on with members of the opposite sex even if you have a boyfriend.

I decided to take a bottle of wine with me from the new French-wine shop, Nicolas, but I was driving so I knew I was only going to have one glass. I'd come straight from work so I was still in my jeans with a baggy shirt tucked in. I deliberately hadn't made a special effort, because why would I? His place wasn't that different to where I live with the rowers, a bit like student digs. The furniture was all kind of mismatched, nothing fancy, a few posters on the wall. Dinner was nice enough, pasta and sauce. I was enjoying the chat, he's an entertaining man with lots of great stories. But after dinner I began to feel a bit uncomfortable. The dynamic changed. He started being a bit suggestive; I think he'd drunk the rest of the bottle over dinner, and another one. There were long silences and he was staring at me a little too long, raising his eyebrows as if to say *when are we going to get started?* It freaked me out and I knew I had to get out of there. That's never happened to me before, the sense of fear that hit me. It felt like my whole system flooded with adrenaline and I pinged up like a shot from the kitchen table and said I was going.

I picked up my bag and walked through his living room to the front door, trying to remain calm. I pulled the lever down on the deadlock and pulled it towards me expecting it to open but it didn't shift. I pulled it again and looking down, realised the door was locked as well. He'd Chubb locked his own front door behind me when I arrived and then taken the key out of the door. What kind of person locks their guests in like that? I scanned the table in the hallway where there were a few things, telephone and address book and post. No keys. He'd got them with him.

I had to shout from the hall: 'Can you let me out please?' My heart was beating so fast.

He very slowly and casually appeared from the dark lounge. He didn't say anything, just leaned on the wall.

'I need to go. Can you unlock the door? Like, now?' I was standing as close to the door as I could, just in case there was any doubt that I wanted to be on the other side of it.

'In a hurry are we?' he asked me, as if I was the one somehow being rude.

'Just let me out, please.'

'All right. Jesus, calm down.'

He took ages going back to the kitchen for the keys. I swear he was doing it deliberately, pretending he couldn't find them. He knew very well where they were.

Everything about this was starting to feel horrible – the air in his house, the emptiness, everything – and I wanted to be out of that place. He did eventually let me out, but the look on his face wasn't pretty when I left. A mix of anger and embarrassment. He didn't like me going at all, the defeat of it.

Never have I loved my car more. I got in and drove home so quickly, I'm sure I went over the speed limit. It wasn't so much an exit as a desperate escape.

At home, safe in my little room at the top of the house, I lay in bed replaying it all in my mind. Should I mention this to anybody at work or not? Did it even really happen? Was I imagining it? Had I made suggestions that he had misread? Was it foolish of me to go for dinner? My legs were shaky, like I needed to run off the energy, and I couldn't sleep for ages. I was dreading going in.

This morning we had a meeting in the office. As we were filing in, he was chatting to a few people, making them laugh as he always does. Suddenly he pointed at me across the whole room and went: 'You! You!' in a pretend menacing way, so that everyone in the room turned around and looked at me.

I had no idea what he was going to say, it was utterly terrifying. I was looking at him without blinking, thinking he was going to say something demeaning, take me down here, in front of everyone. And then he switched into his fun-guy character again, Jekyll and Hyde, and said, 'You've done a fabulous job with television!' Everyone in the meeting was smiling at what a great guy he is. But I knew it was a message. He was telling me I needed to keep my mouth shut.

I don't hate many people, ever, but I hate him now. I'm doing everything I can to stay out of his way. He's all bravado and Mr Big Man but I reckon he probably cries himself to sleep at night. To have to lock someone in when they come for dinner – who feels that insecure about their own company? I can't help but feel angry as well because I feel as though I missed something. And yet I'm sure I didn't make any suggestion that I was interested in him in that way. Because I wasn't. Never will be.

It seems to me that there are some men out there who simply aren't straightforward. In this creative industry bad behaviour is rife. There's a rumour circling that at one of the stations certain male DJs tell pluggers they'll spin their records on the radio in exchange for blow jobs. Thank God I work in television now! With women I always feel I know where I stand. Even if they don't like me, they're either my friend or they're not. But some men seem to like to toy with you, like a kind of cat and mouse game, so you're not sure what you're meant to say or do. There's an agenda. Not all men of course. I'm lucky, most of the men in my life have been transparent, honest, lovely, kind and most importantly trustworthy. I guess that's why it's come as such a shock to encounter a predator like that man. Predator: not a word I thought I'd ever have to use but the cap fits. I'm putting this down as a valuable life lesson. Is proximity to predators the price I have to pay for having such a great job? I sincerely hope not.

Talking about pay, I've been here for over two years now and I know I'm getting results for MCA. I've been thinking about asking for a pay rise and I asked a colleague, a TV and Promotions person, what he thinks I should be pulling in. He's a decent chap and I know I can trust his advice. Get this, he's earning almost double what I am on. OK, he's been there longer than me, but I know that I am getting more exposure on television for our artists than he is. So I decided to see TP about it this afternoon. I didn't go empty-handed because I know by now that you don't go in and just moan about things, no one is interested in me going on about how unfair everything is. I needed to show him facts. So I drew up a graph of all the TV exposure I've secured over the last six months compared to others in the department. I used coloured markers to show their TV slots next to mine and to show exactly how many of my slots could be linked to increased sales, hits for the company. I said to TP: 'I'm not criticising their work, Tony, just demonstrating mine.'

It looked pretty impressive, I have to say. I'm not used to saying I've done well but it was there in black and white. Or should that be coloured markers? It was like being back at school, handing in my homework.

With that kind of evidence in front of him I felt certain that TP would say I could have a pay rise immediately. But instead he shrugged and basically said I had to like it or lump it: 'We might be able to give you a small pay rise but don't get excited, not much is going to change around here any time soon, Nicki.'

And then, just as I was leaving, he added with a wink: 'Oi, why aren't you outside Number 10 waving a copy of Adam Ant's album?'

'Ha, right. I'll get down there right away, boss!' I said, trying to pretend I was joining in the joke. Margaret Thatcher has just resigned. Her leaving Number 10 Downing Street is all over the news. I glance at the TV in Tony's office and see she's looking tearful as she gets in the car with her husband Denis and leaves. The world's press is filming, it's a great PR opportunity for someone, but not Adam Ant.

Back at my desk I'm already wishing I'd pushed back at him a bit, asked him what the rationale behind his thinking is. I wasn't as assertive as I know I could have been. But sometimes I worry that having too much confidence can come across as arrogant or unpleasant. I wish I could be a bit more bullish sometimes. Not always, but it would help in certain situations, not to worry so much about upsetting people. But I also still feel so grateful to have this incredible job. I don't want it to end.

Then just as I was getting ready to go home, a little bit of magic happened. My phone rang:

'Nicki, hi. It's Nick Godwyn over at RCA. Can you talk?'

Why yes, Nick Godwyn at the Radio Company of America, I certainly can.

7

The Only Way Is Up

I slot my CD into my Walkman and enjoy the satisfying clunk as it closes, the disc begins to whirr and those first few tinkly notes of 'Walking on Broken Glass' kick in. It's not out yet, this is an upfront copy of Annie Lennox's new track, top secret and all that. I think it is going to be huge. I sling my new Radley bag over my shoulder, slip into my chunky loafers, admiring the socks I bought from the Sock Shop on Saturday, with the diamond print, and set off on my walk to work.

It is not quite 8 a.m. and the sun is shining on Putney Bridge as I make my way over the Thames. I am practically bouncing my way across, I am feeling so good about life this morning. I am Nicki Chapman, Head of Television at RCA Records.

I'm still getting used to the new environment. The RCA building is nothing like the old MCA offices at Brewer Street. (I know, I could have chosen employers with slightly more different sounding names. There are a lot of three-initial company names in the music industry. Don't ask me why.) It's a proper office block, apparently it used to be the headquarters for Boots. I did want to be a pharmacist when I was younger, so in some ways I've made it. And I guess I do work in an industry known for its use of recreational chemicals! I wonder what Mr Baker, my lovely old boss at the chemist in Herne Bay where I worked on Saturdays, would think of me now?

It's a big brown block of a building; there's nothing much exciting about it, apart from that view across the Thames. I've never worked so close to the river before, something about being right next to it feels energising. It never stops. The offices are still not exactly what I'd call flashy, but it's definitely a step up from MCA. The lifts work here for starters.

How amazing that I get to walk to work and take in this view every morning. It's about fifteen minutes door to door from our house, the dream commute. But I think at some point soon I'd like to move out. I love the rowers, but I want a bigger bedroom and a landline that doesn't need 10-pence coins to operate. So that's my long game here, to save enough for a deposit on a flat. I've been looking in the estate agents in Putney. I should be able to afford something small with what I'm earning now.

Taking this job was a no-brainer after the row about my pay at MCA. First they refused to give me a rise and then a few days later said I could have one, but only because they had decided to let someone else go! Part of me thought I should take the money, but a bigger part of me didn't want to stay on knowing I'd only got it because they'd fired my colleague, not because of the recognition I know I deserved. It was a sloppy seconds pay rise, and it left a nasty taste in my mouth.

Plus, I enjoyed meeting Nick Godwyn so much I felt like it was the right moment to go. Nick took me out for lunch after that call and we had such a good chat, spent hours talking about it all. We're both passionate about music, both love working with creatives and devising campaigns for the label's talent. He is such a lovely, genuine guy, we have definitely connected. It feels like he could be a real mentor, and Lisa Anderson, the MD here, is a woman. I say 'is', apparently she is leaving next week. I was quite keen on the idea of working for a female in the music industry after the last few months at MCA. There aren't many women at that level in the business.

Because Nick found me and called me up and made it so clear that he wanted me to work at RCA, and after kicking myself for not negotiating harder with TP, I felt quite bold about asking for what I wanted my contract to look like. The money is better of course, and I've got a new car, a Golf GTI, and I've been told I can have an assistant at some point.

I also stipulated a couple of very specific things. I thought I might as well. I told Nick that I wanted his guarantee that I'd never be left in a meeting or lunch situation with a couple of male producers I'd worked with the previous year. I won't say who because it might get me into trouble. They are quite high-up producers and I know I'll be dealing with them both now I'm at RCA. Recently I went to the theatre with one of them, a client entertainment kind of thing, and I had to push away a hand on my knee more than a couple of times. Gross. Only on the knee, but that was enough. No way was that paw wandering any higher. The other one was talking about us getting a hotel if they confirmed one of my acts! Really? They were just unacceptable. Vile, even. I don't like them at all. They thought I was easy pickings, and didn't seem to feel embarrassed or ashamed for trying their luck with me. So I told Nick I don't ever want to be left on my own with either of them again, asked him if he could promise me that. He didn't bat an eyelid:

'Yep, not a problem. I promise I will be there at any meetings with them.' I can't decide if it's good he said that or not. It's reassuring to know he has my back. However, if I really think about it, it's also a bit weird. When I ask for that reassurance he automatically accepts it's a peril of the job for a female plugger. It's like Dave Lee Travis (the so-called Hairy Cornflake) over at Radio 1, who always jokes that women shouldn't be left on their own with him in the studio. I'm not sure that is very funny.

Anyway here I am, Head of TV at RCA. The roster here isn't that great at the moment, a bit like MCA in that they don't have any real superstars, and they're not having the success they really want. Black Box is about their biggest name right now. They did 'Ride on Time' in 1989 and 'Everybody, Everybody' was a huge hit in the clubs as well as in the charts. They've got a real Italian house music sound, clubbers love it. But part of the reason they've hired me is to get more exposure for their other artists.

We do have Annie Lennox though, my queen. Now she's left the Eurythmics there's a lot of work going on undercover with her. No one's sure how big she'll be on her own, but I think she'll go stratospheric. I met her manager, a guy called Simon Fuller who runs 19 Entertainment, on my first day. What an interesting man. Very measured and quiet, not like a lot of the managers you meet. He said to me: 'Let me know what I can do to help you, Nicki.' I think that's the first time an artist's manager has ever said that to me. He's impressive.

There's also new label under the RCA umbrella, called Deconstruction, which Kylie is signed to. She left Stock Aitken and Waterman and is developing a much cooler, dance-led sound. I am super-excited about that as well as the other dance and house acts on that label. It feels like there is lots of potential here to go big. The pressure is building, a wave is coming. And I really, really want to be on the crest of it.

The guy who replaced Lisa is called Jeremy Marsh and on first impressions I also like him. He gave us all a talk yesterday, gathered everyone together to introduce himself and said: 'The music industry is about having fun and having success. Anybody here who wants to go home at 5 p.m. every night needs to go and find a job in a bank because this isn't the place for you. We work hard, and we play hard.'

That resonated with me so much. I'm here before 8 a.m. every morning and he often arrives around the same time. We're both early birds catching worms. He's very reassuring. I've spent time around a few different bosses now and I think there are three kinds. You have the boss who believes in you and values your opinion and everything you have to say. You have the slave driver who gets you to do all their work under the guise of 'pushing you'. And you have the negative one who thinks you're always trying to cheat or pull a fast one somehow. Jeremy is the first kind. I know I'm going to love working for him. I have a good feeling about this place.

I call Shelley on my walk home. We're not supposed to make personal calls on the company phone but everyone does. I try to walk to work as much as possible to save money on my travel. Every penny counts now, if I want my own place.

I can't wait to tell Shelley about Annie Lennox on *Wogan* this week. She loves Annie's music as well. We were in the green room together with some of the other guests before Annie was due to go on. The green room is where everyone who appears on a chat show like *Wogan* gathers before and after their appearance. There are always plenty of drinks and snacks, it's meant to be a calm, relaxing space for everyone as very often nerves can be running high when you are about to go on national television. The televisions were on in there, and Annie was standing really close to the screen, watching the news with her hands over her face. Somalia is in the grip of a horrific famine at the moment, thousands of people have died, and the pictures were very distressing, emaciated children and their desperate mothers. You'd have to be made of stone not to feel horrified by it all. The imagery was completely at odds with the room we were in, with all the free food and wine everywhere you turned, and I realised Annie was crying. She was standing there with tears rolling down her face. Just before she was going to go on-screen.

I felt like a terrible person because all I could think was 'How am I going to get her back in the zone? She's going to need to perform in a minute and she's in pieces.' Made up and ready but truly devastated by the news, she was.

What should I say? I had no words. And I'd never dealt with anything like this before.

'What did you do?' Shelley asks.

'I just stood near her and made sure she was given some space. I couldn't do anything else.'

I'm learning that there are certain artists who thrive on having everyone around them fussing and reassuring them, especially before a performance, and there are others who need space and composure. Annie is the latter.

'When I told her we had three minutes, Shell, she didn't

even look at me, she simply took a big breath, wiped her face, lifted her head and suddenly she was there, ready.'

It was an amazing performance, she sang 'Precious' from the new album, standing among classical-style columns all twined with ivy, looking like an actual goddess. Always such a strong, powerful image with Annie.

Then Shelley is straight in there with the important question. 'Anyone catch your eye at work?'

'I wouldn't know, I only have eyes for Greg.' There's a hint of sarcasm in my voice because I'm not sure how long Greg and I are going to last. I'm having an affair with my career at the moment, it's all I can think about. I don't know how I'm meant to find time for Greg, especially now that we don't work together. Although:

'Actually Shell, I did meet someone "quite interesting" today.'

In fact I heard him before I saw him. He was wearing big black cowboy boots with super chunky heels that clicked on the wooden floor in the office. My desk faces the wall so he kind of appeared in front of me and sat right on my desk.

'Hi, I'm Shack, welcome to RCA. I've only just recently joined as well.'

All I could think was how dare this man come and put his buttocks on my desk like that. I pushed back in my seat to let him know I wasn't into his using my desk as a perch for his behind, but he didn't seem to notice and continued with the introductions. I clocked him giving me the once-over: I was wearing my denim shirt and my big cardigan with the shawl collar with the terracottas and blues running through it. I think he appreciated my look, shall we say.

'Hi, I'm Nicki. The new Head of TV.'

He didn't seem to think there was anything wrong with his choice of resting place and continued to sit there with a huge grin on his face. It was hard not to smile right back. He does have a lovely grin, and face.

He's got long sandy-coloured hair and is wearing a leather jacket with tassels on and skin-tight jeans. He clearly loves his rock music. I've since found out that his full name is Dave Shackleton, he's from Yorkshire and he works in marketing, on the international side.

The football results came on the radio while he was sitting there (the radio is pretty much always on) and he turned to me and asked who my team is.

'Well, as you know I've never supported a football team in my life, Shell, but remember when we were little and Dad liked to watch the football, it was always Leeds United who were top of the table, wasn't it? So for some reason I said "Leeds United!"'

'You didn't!'

'I did.'

And I swear to God I saw a light bulb go on in his head. If the denim shirt had drawn him in, it was Leeds United that turned him on.

'Leeds?' he said, addressing no one in particular. 'I'm going to marry this woman.'

8

Could It Be Magic?

I'm in slow-moving traffic, shifting my way back from the BBC studios in Shepherd's Bush to the office in Putney after my meeting. The copy of *Fast Forward* magazine I've been given is open at the centrefold on the passenger seat of my car and I keep glancing over to it. What am I going to do with this? The picture is of five very gorgeous and entirely naked young men with only a few pieces of paper spelling the words TAKE THAT written on their bottoms, providing scant coverage. I can't believe this pic has made it into a teen magazine like *Fast Forward*. Toby Anstis is on the front cover looking like everyone's favourite boy next door; he's the new presenter in the 'Broom Cupboard' on CBBC. That's the kind of story this magazine usually runs. So it's a miracle this picture has made it in at all. But then I'm learning not to be surprised by much in this game.

I've been to the BBC in Wood Lane to see Cathy Gilbey. She's the Executive Producer who works on the main youth and children's entertainment programmes for the BBC. If you want your act on *Going Live!* you need to get Cathy onside first. She's an older lady, in her sixties I think, a former radio journalist who has been working for the BBC for years, and she's something of a legendary figure. She gets the most amazing guests to go on these children's programmes: she put Margaret Thatcher on *Saturday Superstore* once! Hilarious. I like going to her office because there's always a queue of pluggers like me wanting to see her, so I usually bump into someone I know and catch up on the industry gossip. Time with Cathy is golden in this job, so we'll all wait as long as it takes to get a meeting with her. There's no booking system or way of knowing if you'll even get to see her. You just have to turn up and hope. A lot of my week is spent schlepping between here and the RCA offices in Putney hoping to see Cathy and other producers. I call these journeys my pilgrimages. I did them at MCA as well. You just can't beat turning up in person to see someone. It's not the same when you send a bike. When you finally get the nod to go in, Cathy's usually chewing Nicorette gum because she's always trying to give up smoking. She's notorious for giving you short shrift if she doesn't like you, so I always feel I'm one of the lucky ones. I'm very respectful and polite, and I think that goes a long way with our Cathy.

I've come to see her to talk about a new act I'm working on for RCA called M People. I want to get them on *Going Live!* with Phillip Schofield and Sarah Greene. It's the most popular Saturday-morning kids' show at the moment. They have a hilarious double act, Trevor and Simon, who do a slot called 'Singing Corner' where they get the special guest to sing a song with them, usually while they're dressed up in something strange or doing something silly. They had Cliff Richard on singing 'Summer Holiday' and they made him hold a lilo and threw beach balls at his head. It's clownish and very funny; mums and dads like Trevor and Simon as much as the kids do. And everyone appearing knows it's part of the deal – on Saturday afternoons everyone goes shopping and buys your single because they've seen you on *Going Live!*. Well, not all artists. Apparently Bros turned it down recently because they want to be taken more seriously.

I wanted to talk to Cathy about getting M People on there when their new single comes out. But before I could even get a word in she pushed this copy of *Fast Forward* towards me, open at the centre, and says: 'Look at this! Look at this!'

And there were these naked young men, a group from Manchester called Take That. I've seen the video of their song called 'Do What U Like' where it's basically them dancing around in a white studio with black leather sort of cycle shorts on, getting covered in jelly or shaving foam or something else and a girl wiping a broom up and down their bottoms. Nice work if you can get it. The song was OK but it hadn't charted. Radio just hadn't given it any airtime, and without that it's super hard to break a new act.

I looked at Cathy. 'Seriously?'

And she said, thumping their bottoms with her pen as she spoke: 'Yes! This! This! This! This would be amazing on the show! Look at them. Boy band, boy band material. Cheeky chappies, northern. Love it. Look at them. Look at them, Nicki.' I stood there, incredulous. This was so far away from anything I had come prepared to talk about.

'I'm fed up with all these faceless dance acts, they're no good on television. I want a band with personality. Go and find them, Nicki. Go and find them.'

So now I'm sitting in traffic on the Fulham Palace Road wondering what I can do with this. I've got a golden ticket from Cathy Gilbey at the BBC, if I can get Take That on my roster, I know she'll put them on Saturday-morning TV. The UK certainly needs a decent boy band, but how do I get to them? I'm not in the A&R business, I'm the plugger, I deal with the finished product, not the bare beginnings. 'Scuse the pun.

I keep looking at the picture, chuckling. It's so shamelessly naughty. You certainly can't forget them once you've seen it. An idea is starting to form in my mind and when I get back to the office, finally, I go around all the desks and main areas and pick up all the copies of *Fast Forward* I can find. People are always dashing around here with magazines and bits of paper in their hands, no one seems to notice or wonder what

I'm doing. Back at my desk I gently pull each staple up so that I can ease the centrefold from each copy, without tearing the image in a crucial spot. Then I head straight to the A&R department and stick copies of Take That's naked bottoms on the doors to all the offices. Artist and Repertoire are the talent seekers – if anyone can get hold of this lot, they can – but I need to get their attention. The picture is so arresting and Cathy has been so explicit in her desire to get these boys on television, I need to at least try to engineer a meeting.

After about ten minutes Nick Raymond, one of the A&R team, calls me to his office and asks what on earth this door poster is about. After we have both stopped laughing and wondering what has possessed me, I say:

'Nick, you have to get me that act. I know I can get them on television. They can obviously sing. They've had a single out and have done a video. I will get them a slot on prime Saturday-morning television if you can sign that act.'

'Well, Nicki, you are in luck,' he says. 'You won't believe this but we are already in talks with their manager. It's looking like we're about to sign them.'

Nick says that the group has been put together in Manchester by the owner of a modelling agency up there, a man called Nigel Martin-Smith. Apparently, he's very successful and has decided he wants to put together a boy band. It was his dream to create one, so that's what he's done. No record companies have been involved until now. He's used his connections on the gay club circuit, held auditions, self-funded the video for 'Do What U Like', and Gary, the lead singer, wrote the song. He can't be any older than nineteen. Can you believe that? It's an amazing story. Nigel must be a pretty impressive guy to have the passion and vision to put this together with no experience. A whole video and a centre-page spread in *Fast Forward* and it was all purely this man. Someone told me there's five of them in case one leaves, which makes sense when you think about it. Unfortunately for them the track died a death, but for a first single that's quite normal in this game. And the cheeky centrespread got everyone's attention. It certainly got Cathy's. So now here we are. Nick says he's coming in to the office next week with the band.

'Well, your TV's sorted, Nick,' I say to him over my shoulder as I leave his office. I don't want there to be any doubt in his mind about what signing Take That will mean. 'We'll be well away. Sign them.'

This is what I've been waiting for. My first boy band.

9

Tell Me What You Want

I'm lugging my haul up the stairs to my new flat. I've been down to Hammersmith after work and picked up a few more bits. I stop on the landing to swap the bags over because they're so heavy. I didn't realise I would need to buy all this stuff! Everything was there when I moved in with the rowers, but I don't have anything of my own, not even a mug, so I'm having to buy literally everything new. It's a good job I like shopping. I've got this amazing dried flower wreath to go above my bed, it smells of lavender and roses and I think it might be my favourite thing ever.

I've bought the top flat in a Victorian terrace, not quite as big as the house with the rowers, but in the same kind of style. It's only a one-bedroom flat but it's all on the same floor. Being at the top of the house seems to be a theme with me. I've got a little kitchen, living room, my bedroom and my bijoux bathroom in the eaves. All mine. I love the view from in there in the morning, I feel like Mary Poppins up among all the London roofs and chimneys. If I squint I can see the old house from here, so I don't feel too far away from my rowers. Greg is only down the road as well. And of course I can still walk to work.

I got the keys at the weekend and Greg helped me move my stuff in. I've had a new pine bed and chest of drawers de-livered from the nice furniture shop on the Lower Richmond Road in Putney, and I bought myself new coffee, tea and sugar jars from British Home Stores when I was home last weekend at Mum's picking up a few things. They're cream with black writing. And some glass salad plates in the shape of a leaf, which I love. People ask me if I'm going to mind living by myself, but honestly I am in heaven. This is going to be my sanctuary. I've been saving for this place for a long time. It feels like every penny has been going towards this moment and it is finally mine.

I'm off to *Top of the Pops* this evening and I am going out for dinner afterwards with my boss Nick, Annie Lennox and Simon, her manager. We're going to the Japanese we all like on the Finchley Road. As luck would have it, eating out is a major part of my job. The long boozy lunches I remember with Phil and the gang at MCA don't happen so much these days. It's hard to believe that just a few years ago it was perfectly normal for the whole department to disappear for 'lunch' and leave me in charge of the place. But taking our artists and their management out to eat is still very much a thing and choosing the right place is becoming an art form in itself. Eating out is no longer simply about eating; where you go is definitely starting to mean something. There are whole magazines devoted to restaurant reviews, like with music. London's restaurant scene is booming and there are great new places opening up all over the city. Nobu, The Atlantic, Le Caprice. There's a great Belgian place that serves moules frites and the waiters are all dressed as monks. Some chefs are even developing their own reputations, like pop stars, or should I say rock'n'roll stars. Marco Pierre White apparently has a very short temper and throws any journalists he doesn't like out of his restaurant, Harveys. I haven't been there yet but it's definitely on the list.

Japanese is still my favourite and always a treat; the place we're going tonight does amazing sashimi. Who knew I'd love raw fish so much? It's a long way from the Friday-night fish and chips of Herne Bay. The restaurant isn't fancy by any stretch, low key but with sensational food. I've been there quite a few times with my artists on the way home from filming *Top of the Pops*. They always get the choice of where to go, and I'm happy to oblige. Another regular haunt is the Japanese at the Kensington Hilton. I say Kensington, but it's right on the roundabout of Shepherd's Bush – or Shey-Boo as some of the locals call it. It's a stone's throw from Wood Lane where nearly all the BBC programmes are made. Hey, if my artists want Japanese for lunch, I'm not about to stop them. It beats the Beeb canteen any day.

Annie has been on *Top of the Pops* this evening, performing a track from her new album. I was secretly quite relieved all had gone smoothly as I'd had to sweet-talk my way in after a bit of a to-do with another of my current artists, Gary Clail. He had a great track out recently, 'Human Nature', which got to number 10 in the charts and was really popular in the clubs. I had him booked on to *Top of the Pops*, to perform with his keyboard player and a rather flamboyant singer called Alan Pellay, who did the vocals in this wonderfully deep, sexy voice. Gary and the keyboard player were both in plain black garb, they looked a bit underwhelming to be honest. But Alan, who sometimes also goes by the name Lana, was all dressed up in colourful regalia with a big turban covered in fruit, and huge swathes of brightly coloured silk. I thought it was a fab look, it really brightened up the stage. Rehearsals were going smoothly in the afternoon before the show, when over the tannoy I heard the words:

'Nicki Chapman to the gallery please. Nicki Chapman to the gallery immediately.'

The gallery is where the producer sits, it's like a mezzanine floor over the studio so they can see everything that is going on below. I opened the door and the producer, Paul Ciani, who I had only recently repaired my relationship with after Bobby Brown, span around in his chair and practically spat the words out: 'What the fuck is that on my stage? This isn't some camp pantomime show. Get fucking Carmen Miranda out of my studio now!'

I was quite surprised as I know Paul is gay and I naively assumed he'd be all for a bit of kitsch, but he was clearly quite angry and definitely not happy about it. I went downstairs and quietly explained to Gary and Alan that the fruity turban and the colourful robes would sadly need to go, and thankfully they were very understanding. Alan dashed back to the dressing room and re-emerged in a plain black suit, matching Gary's black anorak, and only a sequinned headscarf as a nod to any fabulousness. I wasn't blacklisted again, but it was a difficult moment and I was worried it might make things harder for me with other acts on the show.

Fortunately Annie Lennox is a goddess and Paul had been very gracious about having her on. She did an incredible performance and we've come here to have dinner and decompress afterwards. There's a great atmosphere around the table because the pressure is off and we are all a little bit demob happy. It also helps that Nick and Annie get on like a house on fire. They have real chemistry and they are laughing at each other all evening. I'm sitting next to Simon, who I've been getting to know better over the last few weeks, as we are working together on Annie and a couple of his other acts. He's got such a calm way about him – quietly spoken, considered – and he listens very intently as we chat. I feel he's someone who is going to teach me so much and I'm going to enjoy working with him. I mean, this is the guy who signed Madonna to Chrysalis with 'Holiday' and gave Paul Hardcastle his N-n-n-n-nineteen hit. He's already a legend in my book.

Not long after I joined RCA he booked a meeting room for us and talked me through everything that was happening with Annie Lennox and his vision for her and what she wants as an artist. No manager has ever done that with me before and I've realised it's so important, if we are going to get the promotion right, to give me a clear understanding of their work, the direction they want to go in creatively. Otherwise I could go off in one direction when artistically they're going somewhere else.

'She's been away for a couple of years after the Eurythmics but is going all out on her own now,' he explained. 'She's got incredibly strong visuals, very committed to her own style and artistic integrity.'

Annie is a very principled artist, he said, very strong and measured, thoughtful. 'She's passionate about her music, can be quite political and has her own views about the music industry, but for all the right reasons.'

All of this is catnip to me of course. I already adore Annie Lennox so this is the icing on the cake. I cannot wait to work with her, it's going to be a huge honour. I've been working with a lot of kids' shows recently, with artists like Take That, which is always fun and definitely has its purpose. But with Annie it's all about the voice and her songwriting. It's a different league.

Now I'm sitting here opposite her in a Japanese restaurant, feeling like it's the most natural thing in the world – well, nearly – and being quite pleased with myself about how well I can handle my chopsticks these days. She and Nick are deep in a conversation about someone they both know and just as I squeeze a big piece of salmon into my mouth, I feel Simon's gaze turn towards me.

'So come on, tell me what you want.'

'Hey?' I say, trying not to let the wasabi that is burning my mouth impair my speech too much.

'Tell me what you really want. What does the industry need? In your opinion I mean. What would really fly if I found it for you?'

This is what makes Simon Fuller so great to work with and so different. He genuinely values my opinion and experience.

He's asked me so I tell him. 'Well Simon, I've got my boy band, I've got Take That. Now I need girls.' I explain that ever since the day Wendy James came into the office at MCA and made Phil roar with laughter, it has struck me how few really strong female-led acts we have. Annie Lennox is amazing but I'm thinking more about a band aimed at the teenage market. Kylie is great, an actress, literally the girl next door. Where are all the feisty, powerful young women, like Wendy, and like Debbie Harry used to be? There's a girl group called Eternal. Their music is well-produced and riding the charts. But they don't quite have the charisma or edge I'm after: the strong image I'm thinking of, that I know has such a big impact. I want talent, as well as strong characters that I can really work with.

'So, yeah, Simon, I guess what I really, really want is a dynamic girl group.'

10

Them Girls, Them Girls

Have I just been spat at? Really? Bloody hell. That makes me furious, it really does. 'Who did that?' I am shouting into the darkness. The sun isn't up yet.

I stop to check it didn't actually land on me. I heard it but I can't see where it went. It had better not have, this is a new coat (from Whistles, thank you, I do love a coat). As I'm patting myself down someone shouts: 'You fucking bitch!'

I'm really not in the mood for this. It's 6 a.m. and I am cold and tired and I want a cuppa and some breakfast. I turn around to face the crowd of girls who are all braying at me from behind the fence. I've got no way of knowing which one spat at me so I address all of them:

'You know what girls, that is not ladylike at all. Not at all. Do you want me to tell the boys that's how you behave?'

The group screams in panic, as one. 'No! No! Please don't tell them. We love you, Nicki! Sorry!'

I feel myself softening a little. These poor girls. It's the middle of February, for crying out loud, and they're all here in their uniforms, standing by a damp canal before they go to school, hoping to catch a glimpse of Take That. If they actually ever get to school.

'Look, I'm not a threat girls, you have absolutely nothing to worry about with me, OK? I'm just doing my job here. But please, be nice. Or I'll tell the boys.'

A girl shouts: 'Can you give this to Robbie for his birthday? Please?' I make out a fluffy red heart toy with a balloon attached to it and what looks like a very long letter in an envelope. They are relentlessly optimistic, I'll give them that.

'No, sorry, I can't! Have a great day, girls!'

I turn and walk over the little bridge to the other side of the canal, down the alleyway and through the back gate of the house where *The Big Breakfast* is filmed. I've been here every morning this week. It's all the way over in Bow, east London, so I am up at 4 a.m. to get across the city to be here for 6 a.m. The presenter, Chris Evans, is away this week and I've managed to get Take That standing in for him all week with Gaby Roslin. It's the Take That Takeover!

They were on *The Big Breakfast* a few weeks ago, singing in the shower with Chris and Zig and Zag. How do I describe Zig and Zag? They're a pair of crazy kind of alien Rastafarian puppets who apparently come from the planet

Zog but talk with Irish accents. They're not real (obviously) but are performed by a couple of Irish guys. Simon Cowell signed them to RCA, along with the Power Rangers and a few other novelties. Not exactly the hippest artists on our roster. But Simon doesn't mind if people laugh at him, he's so thick-skinned, always with a smile and the wink of an eye. I can actually see Zig and Zag doing well, people love them.

All the boys in Take That are natural showmen in their own different ways, you can throw anything at them. They did so well singing in the shower that morning that having them as guest presenters was an easy yes from the production team. Today is the last day of their week here. It also happens to be the last show before Valentine's Day, which is in two days' time, and not only that but it is Robbie's birthday tomorrow. No wonder every teenage girl in the land is here.

It works having five of them; it fits with the 'zoo' TV format so many of the programmes are based on these days. Zoo is where you have a central presenter, or two (or five, if it happens to be Take That), who are joined throughout the show by various regular people and features. Everything is a little bit loose and unpredictable. I suppose it's like seeing all the different animals in a zoo. It's been common in radio for a while: think of Steve Wright with his Old Woman, Mick Jagger and Elvis characters. But now it's the way so many of the television shows work as well, especially the youth programmes, anything with Chris Evans in it. *The Big*

Breakfast is all filmed at an old pumping station in what was once a proper house near London's old docklands. There's nothing around it for miles, it's surrounded by wasteland, so it's probably quite cheap to lease.

Because it's filmed in an old house rather than a conventional studio, it's always freezing cold. All the doors and windows are open with thousands of feet of wires and leads running through. It's not like an airtight studio with designated make-up rooms and production galleries – you have to walk through the actual house to do anything. Often you are treading over cables and sets, people will be walking past you with chairs. Someone shouting from the kitchen: 'Does anyone want a bacon butty?' There are cable bashers running around the place because most of the camerawork is done on a handheld camera going up and down the stairs.

As a show it's chaotic and messy and noisy. It has shaken up breakfast television with its standard studio format and has developed a huge following. I would say it is groundbreaking television in every sense. A lot of young people and young adults love it. There's news, but they keep it swift and tongue in cheek. The headlines say things like 'More Bad News'. Paula Yates does a regular feature where she interviews people on a giant bed in her nightie and you can see she has no underwear on. Hilarious. Does she never get cold? I'm always frozen in that place. I'm thinking the boys can come back and do the segment with her at Christmas maybe, although I'm not sure it's a good idea. I love Paula but she's like an octopus around people on that bed and they may enjoy it a bit too much. And I think she's got her eye on one of them.

Being spat at is not cool. I didn't sign up for this, although it's not the first time I've been on the receiving end of un-wanted bodily fluids in the name of my work. Once when I was still at MCA I was opening some post for Kim Wilde. Kim is one of those artists everyone fancies, men and women. She is naturally sexy, a gorgeous woman, but so self-effacing. She had some huge hits in the early 1980s in-cluding 'Kids In America' and was back with a bang. When I was at MCA she was making a small comeback. I think that's the first time I realised artists can have peaks and troughs, like the rest of us. It's not always a straightforward trajectory to fame and fortune. That was when Phil, bless him, took me to see her supporting Michael Jackson. In fact she's been a guest presenter on *The Big Breakfast* recently as well. I think Chris Evans really fancied her. Anyway at MCA we used to get all sorts sent to the office marked for Kim's attention: people sending in pictures and asking for her number and so on. One morning I put my hand in a padded envelope and pulled out a sachet of what I quickly realised was cold semen. Loads of it. Someone had been very busy thinking about Kim. The little bag it was in wasn't secured properly and it spilled out and went all up my arm. Absolutely dis-gusting. I was hysterical, so Graham let me go home early to have a shower and get changed. Thank God someone else opens the post these days. I hope they're more careful than I was.

I'm glad this week is over. It's been fun but also so busy, what with going to the house every day, and there's a new tour to plan and prepare for. The band has an entourage now and it's my job to keep the whole thing running smoothly. There's Paul and James the security guys, Jennie on hair and Bonnie the stylist. You'd imagine Take That would be quite light on the styling – they're not like some female acts that need hours in hair and make-up – but with five of them there's still always a lot of wardrobe and clothes. Styling, wardrobe, hair, make-up, this is all a new experience for me. Plus there's Ying, the band's brilliant assistant, they all love Ying. Then there's Mark, the good-looking make-up guy, and of course Nigel. They go back a long way, and they are always bickering about something. One day when we were filming *What's Up Doc?* with Pat Sharp in Maidstone, they had a huge barney in a hotel room. It sounded like all the furniture was being moved around. I knocked on the door and asked if everything was OK. Mark and Nigel looked rather sheepish. Tensions can get very high on the road.

Everywhere we go, every gig, every journey, I have to make sure all of these people know where they're going, what they're doing and when. That they all get something to eat and have somewhere to sleep and a means of getting from A to B. It's pretty heavy on the logistics sometimes. I'm like a circus ringmaster. I give them all itineraries, sometimes known as call sheets. These have all the details they need: addresses, telephone numbers, names and places. I give them each a call sheet before we do anything, always in a clear plastic folder. And then I usually give them another one, or two, as they often lose them. It's stressful and hectic, but also hugely rewarding, to be the stability for them, the one who they can ask. It sounds cheesy but it feels like a family and I love it.

Of course the difference for me is I can go home at night. Or if we are overseas I can go home when my work is done. I'm not in the band (that would be an error) and I'm not required at every show. So I'm not sharing hotel rooms with them, having to be around everyone 24/7. I know that can be hard; it's hard even for the greatest friends. I know I could get fed up with my friends after two weeks on holiday with them! Mind you, sometimes work and holidays blur into one. I organised for Level 42 to appear on a GMTV special, *Fun in the Sun*, recently. The whole show was broadcast from the beach in Torremolinos. The boys had decided to buy the worst nylon Hawaiian shirts they could find for their performance. They'd entered into the spirit of things, hit the tiles the night before and thought these outfits were hilarious. As they were getting ready to go on stage, or should that be sand, hordes of drunk Brits began traipsing past as they made their way home from the clubs. All dragging themselves back to their apartments, sunburnt and clutching cans of lager.

Mark King looked at me just before he went on and said from the side of his mouth: 'And thus endeth an illustrious career.' I grew up with a major crush on this man and now I was standing on a beach in Torremolinos with him and the band dressed up like tour reps. They saw the funny side, while I was mortified to have put them through it. The things I ask people to do for the sake of publicity.

I adore Level 42. I also adore the Take That boys. Every one of them. They know they can trust me because I've been here from the start, ever since that chat with Cathy and the day we got them signed. It's so different when you are with an act from the start, you put down roots together.

That was so funny, when they came in for that first meeting at RCA, they were all sat on the sofa outside Nick Raymond's office and of course I knew who they were – I'd even seen their bare bottoms – but they had no clue who I was. Howard is only a few years younger than me so we're not years apart age-wise either. I was wearing heels that day (someone in the office calls them my fuck-me shoes, cheeky sod) and I trotted into Nick's office, walked right past them and could feel their collective gaze on me as I went in. I couldn't help but have a little smile to myself, thinking *you wait fellas, you're going to realise I'm your publicist soon!*

Now we have a major boy band on the books and I'm managing their television and promotions. My first boy band. It hasn't all been plain sailing and certainly hasn't happened overnight. There was lot of work behind the scenes to get to a point where the 'general public' were engaged with Take That. They worked so hard touring the gay and under-eighteen clubs at first, the pink pound being just as important as the teenage girls with this lot – just look at them, in their little cycling shorts and studded leather belts. Nigel, their manager, who I find very entertaining and have so much fun with, worked so hard at building their fan base. He's like a mother hen; he really cares and views the band as his extended family. But he also rules them with an iron fist. As he's financed them from the start, I guess he feels he has a sense of ownership over them. Once when Jason was running late for a cover shoot for *My Guy* magazine, Nigel let it go ahead without him – refused to wait and let him take part. They had to add his face on afterwards. He always refers to Jason as the painter and decorator, to remind him where he came from. You wouldn't want to mess with Nigel, but equally he's a passionate manager and always working so hard for the boys. He started collecting names and addresses at the end of their shows so that we can send information to the fans about new releases and so on. Such a clever idea, we've never really used that kind of direct marketing tech-nique before, it's so simple and a very efficient way to build loyalty and stay in touch with fans.

Their first single with RCA was 'Promises'. It was a fab high-energy track, co-written by Gary, and we knew the gay community would embrace it as much as the girls. But Radio 1 and the regional stations weren't that interested in it. It's really tough to break a new band on radio, without the image to support the sound. I knew TV would be the thing to launch them. So I talked to Peter Estall, the Executive Producer at *Wogan*, and he was very taken with them. We had lunch and over coffee he said:

'You know what, Nicki? We're going to give these young chaps a go. Why don't we give them the biggest break of their life? *Wogan* has a reputation for having established acts on but we also like to nurture new talent.'

This was the stuff of dreams for me as their promotions manager. Getting an unknown boy band onto the country's most popular television show is quite an achievement, especially given the current competition. I know I would have been up against some seriously big acts to get this spot for the boys. The days of Stock Aitken and Waterman acts dominating every show are thankfully starting to fade, but still, the charts are packed with talent right now: Bryan Adams, Boyz II Men, Paula Abdul, Jesus Jones. The list of brilliant alternatives to this unknown boy band from Manchester is almost endless. But I did it. Their first major TV performance and it was *Wogan*.

We had rehearsals for a couple of days in a nearby studio. Howard and Jason were both dancers on *The Hit Man and Her*, so they choreographed the whole routine for the band. It was very energetic, lots of head spins and back flips, although not for Gary as he was doing a live vocal. The first time they walked into the BBC studio in Wood Lane, on the day, it was a treat to see their faces. You watch *Wogan* at home and you think you know what the studio looks like but in real life it's completely different. The area where Terry sits to interview the guests is very small but on the other side there's an enormous set and when you look up it seems to have no ceiling. It goes up and up. There are huge black 'flats', big panels that can be moved to create the performance area, and reams of cables running along the floors and up into the gantries above, where lighting technicians and other production people scurry around. There are make-up artists with their big over-the-shoulder bags full of make-up, hair and wardrobe people milling around. Sound guys putting mics on. It's like walking into a little village, bustling with life. I looked at the boys, so excited and full of nerves for the show. They definitely weren't in Kansas any more.

The styling was quite racy for *Wogan*. They were in leather trousers and waistcoats, some with no top underneath and others with shirts open. I'd had big Take That signs made for each side of the stage, there was purple lighting and the dry ice was pumping. They looked brilliant and delivered 110 per cent with their performance. Quite a few of their fans had made it in to the show as well so there was a palpable thrill in the atmosphere, something you don't always get in a studio performance.

After the show I took them all to the Hard Rock Cafe and Robbie – bless him, he was still only sixteen – turned to me and said: 'You know what, Nicki? I reckon I've made it. I'm sixteen years of age and I've been on *Wogan*. And if it all ends tomorrow, how great is that?'

I don't think I'll ever forget that conversation, it was so endearing and he was so young and excited. I looked at them there having the time of their lives because the burgers were free and they'd been on *Wogan*, and I felt sure we were, all of us, on the verge of something incredible. And then the single was released. 'Promises' peaked at number 38 in the charts. Not even top 20. Flopped. Everyone was devastated. So much time, effort and money had gone into it by that point. I'd secured them interviews and performances on the biggest television show in the UK, as well as Saturday-morning kids' TV. They're gorgeous, full of personality, write their own songs. All the right ingredients were there and it just hadn't connected. We talk about 'getting things away' in plugging, and somehow we hadn't got it away.

There were, unsurprisingly, rumblings from the top about how much more the company would invest in this act. Would the band now be dropped? I couldn't imagine it. They were clearly destined for the top in my eyes. But then I'm not the one holding the purse strings. I knew my job was going to get tougher. I'd have to go back to them and say, 'We haven't had a hit but let's try again, shall we?' And that's what we did. We went back to the independent local radio stations and plugged away at them. Sent the band on a tour of the regional stations, got them jumping out of a van and doing impromptu a cappella performances in the street. It could have been a nightmare with a different band, definitely not something I could ask of certain people, but the boys are so positive and full of energy. And they really appreciate their fans. They're not snooty about them at all like some artists can be. They always take lots of time signing a myriad of things – bras, dummies, sandwiches, CD cases, the occasional patch of cleavage – and chatting to the girls afterwards.

We had yet another single that didn't make it into the top 20, 'Once You've Tasted Love'. And then, finally, with 'It Only Takes A Minute', they did it, straight in at number 7. It was a genius move to have them do a disco track. RCA had been getting the jitters about the viability of the band and there was some debate about the appeal of Gary's songwriting, so it was decided by those on high that a cover version of a 1970s disco song would be the way to the top of the charts. Everyone loves disco, don't they? The music press loved it. The gay clubs loved it. And of course by then, Take That's fans had formed an army – the TTs – and nothing could hold them back.

11

I Think We're Alone Now

'I got them.'

Simon Fuller is on the phone, sounding very excited.

'Got what?'

'I got the girl band.'

'I'm sorry?'

'The girl group you wanted. I've found them and you're going to love them.'

I take a moment to sift through my memories. It's easy to lose track sometimes with so much going on.

It clicks.

'Do you mean what we were talking about with Annie that time?'

'Yes! You said you wanted to work with a dynamic girl group and I've found them. They're sensational.'

Well, this is interesting. Simon explains that he's been to watch this group of girls perform. They're all living together in a house somewhere in the south of England having been put together by a father-and-son team of talent managers, but apparently the girls are unhappy with the way they're being managed. They sound like they have their own minds, which is good to hear. Simon's bringing them over to him at 19 Entertainment on a development deal, putting them in the studio with some good writers to develop their sound. When the time is right he says he'll take them around the labels and decide which one to go with. Obviously, it would be great if he'd bring them to RCA.

'I'll keep you in the loop, send you some tracks when I get some. I really want you to work with them, Nicki.'

I put the phone down slowly and take a moment to process this. It means a lot that he has so much faith in me. This is the difference with Simon Fuller, he actually does what he says he's going to do. I believe him, they will be sensational. I'm looking forward to seeing them. I wonder what they're like? But for now, I have to square that away somewhere in the back of my mind and focus on Take That. There is so much to think about. They are pretty much always on promo tours these days and I'm lucky enough to go along with them as much as I can. I've been to Japan, Australia, the States and all over Europe as part of the entourage. We usually fly business class and there is always a group of fans waiting to greet them when they land. The boys are great travellers, although it's not always easy to drag them away from the gorgeous and highly enthusiastic welcome committee.

I don't stay for all of the dates, because I've still got a job here at RCA and a long list of other artists to think about: Kylie Minogue, Level 42, Rick Astley, SWV, Morrissey, London Beat, Michelle Gayle, and Felix, to name a few. But I always do what I need to do for the boys. I take out film crews, set up interviews and work with the international promo team in these territories. It's not always easy in a foreign country, but a huge perk of all this travel for the team (and me) is trying the local food. Our palates are changing already. A few years ago a Chinese takeaway was about the most exotic food we'd experienced, now the boys are quaffing saké like it's going out of fashion and they all know what they want to order without looking at the menu. They're still young, and travelling is a brand new experience for them, and me, so I try to make sure it's not just a case of fly in, perform and out again. They can engage with their international audiences better when they understand the country they're in a little more. Although truthfully, often when they're exhausted what they want is a burger and fries in their hotel rooms. Howard especially loves his coffee and always puts on his broadest Manc accent to make me laugh. 'Nikkeh, I want a coffeh.' Home comforts become more important when you're away so much. Jason always brings his much-loved guitar with him wherever we go. Gary likes to joke: 'He'll learn to play it one day.' I know I love coming back to my little flat, my sanctuary. I'm such a philistine, I always want to eat sausage and mash when I get home.

The boys are having the time of their lives and I am still pinching myself that I get to be part of it.

Everyone asks me if I party with them. Do we stay up late and hit the town and go wild? What goes on tour stays on tour and all that. Sometimes. I have a Triple A pass, which means I have access everywhere when they are performing: wardrobe, catering, hair and make-up, underneath the stage, in the coaches. I am everywhere with them. So yes, we do hang out, we have great fun, there's always a few drinks afterwards, or we go out for dinner. What they get up to later is down to them, as long as manager Nigel doesn't find out. These are the moments I enjoy most, when they are relaxed and telling their stories, things the fans have said to them. But I've always got one eye on the time, so I'm rarely there till the end. Robbie's usually the last one standing of course. He's the one we're always waiting for – he sleeps in too late, disappears off and we have to track him down. I'm definitely honing my detective skills.

Recently we were filming *Top of the Pops* at Elstree studios. I was there helping them get sorted before the show started when I realised Robbie was nowhere to be seen. I went up and down the corridors knocking on doors. Eventually I found him in a dressing room with, let's just say, a member of the cast of *EastEnders*. The whole Walford/*EastEnders* set is at Elstree so there's always someone from Albert Square wandering around. It's funny when you're in the bar there and Pauline Fowler and Mrs Hewitt wander in like best friends. Interestingly enough, Arthur Fowler is nowhere to be seen. The boys were a bit star-struck at first; they've all grown up watching *EastEnders*. Somehow Robbie had ended up in a cupboard in this young lady's dressing room and was looking very pleased with himself when I found him. 'Busy are we?' I said as he emerged, rearranging his outfit. I love him but he is always the one giving me a headache.

That's the other thing people ask me: do the boys hook up with their fans much? They're young lads and this is the music industry. Certainly when we are travelling they like to experience the local 'culture', shall we say. But quite honestly they don't do it when I'm there. What I do see is that they really care about the 'Thatters' or the 'TTs', as their fans are known. They always take time to chat and sign as many things as they can. They know many of them by name. Even when they're exhausted and just want to get home they always make time.

Some of them have more fans than others. Gary jokes because he knows he's not the most fancied one, but he doesn't mind. He says, with a smile on his face: 'I can get inside, get changed and have a brew. Mark's going to be out here for hours.' Although the fans are becoming more and more difficult to manage. I reckon teenage girls would make brilliant spies. They seem to know where and when the boys are going to be and they somehow manage to turn up in the strangest places. Mark went home to see his parents recently and there were girls on a ladder at the front window of his mum's house, trying to look in through the gap at the top of the curtains. On a recent trip to Newcastle, girls were standing outside the hotel singing Take That hits all night. I went to sleep listening to them and when I woke up they were still going strong. You can hear 'Promises' one too many times. I haven't been close up to this kind of teenage mania before. It's thrilling and exciting to witness the passion. And of course, the teenager market is the lifeblood of this industry. Anyone who overlooks their importance and their sway in making or breaking a band does so at their peril. But as I always say, I can walk away when I want to. For the band it is constant.

Looking back, I think the first hint I had that it was going to be like this was after that initial gig they did on *Wogan*. We'd sent a mailer to the fan base saying something like 'If you're a Take That fan, do you want to come down to the studio and watch?' It was great because we had loads of girls screaming in the audience. I'm not sure Terry knew what was going on. But after the show, as we left, two things happened that made me realise something big was afoot. Driving out of the iconic horseshoe-shaped drive at the BBC in Shepherd's Bush, I had their manager Nigel in the car with me. The band was in a separate car. We were going to the Hard Rock Cafe to celebrate. As I was edging out, hordes of girls suddenly swamped my car, banging on it, whacking on the door. It really terrified me because it came out of nowhere.

They all had the Take That logo painted on their faces and their T-shirts, like warriors. All of them were trying to take pictures inside the car with their disposable cameras. The band hadn't even had a hit yet! I said to Nigel: 'Oh my God, oh my God, what do I do?'

'Just keep driving. Keep driving slowly.'

I edged forward very slowly but the girls weren't moving, the car was surrounded. Suddenly I heard a 'boof' and re-alised I had hit one of them. I was going so slowly she was OK, but it was a scary moment. I could have hurt her. She, however, didn't bat an eyelid. I opened the window slightly to see if she was OK and before I could say anything she screamed at me: 'Where's the band?'

'They're in the other car,' I said. And off she ran.

It was frightening, because I'd never seen that kind of hysteria before. I think the closest I had come to it would have been the shopping centre tour we did with Tiffany when I was at MCA. Remember Tiffany, with all the red hair? Her song 'I Think We're Alone Now' was a huge hit in both the UK and the US, in 1988. Tiffany came over from America and she was doing a shopping mall tour around the country, because all the teenagers are usually there on Saturday afternoons, in the Pavilions or the Trocadero or their nearest big shopping centre. They hang out in HMV or Our Price, listening to music on the headphones, or trying on perfumes in places like the Body Shop. They're too young for nightclubs and concerts are expensive, so we took the acts to them in shopping centres. It doesn't happen so much now but there was a period in the late 80s where it felt like we had someone on in a shopping centre somewhere every weekend. I had been given the green light to go along to the Eldon Square shopping centre in Newcastle with Freddo, the Artist Liaison, who was always kind about letting me tag along, even though I was still a secretary at that point. So many people had turned up to see Tiffany play outside Virgin Records that it had become a bit of a riot. Thousands of teens showed up because it wasn't ticketed, so free for all. Eventually they had to close all the shops and lock the doors until the mall was empty. Little Tiffany was there among all those screaming fans, with no security or anything. Her manager wasn't around – apparently he had to fly to Europe – so we were left with a sixteen-year-old artist to look after.

The following weekend, as part of that same shopping mall tour, Freddo and I went with Tiffany and her UK promoter, Harvey Goldsmith (who also happens to be the man who put on Live Aid in 1985), to the Trocadero in London's Leicester Square, for another live performance and a signing. The Troc was the place to be for teenagers in London back then. It had cinemas and shops and arcades, as well as a Guinness Book of Records exhibition. SegaWorld had yet to open there, but it was already a hub for video gamers. Kids hung out there all day. Due to the sheer numbers waiting to see Tiffany perform we went in via the service entrance in Shaftesbury Avenue. Tiffany, Freddo, Harvey Goldsmith and I went up in a big service lift to the top floor, where all the restaurants were and where Tiffany would be performing. Suddenly the lift stopped. We pressed all the buttons but after a few minutes a voice came over the intercom to say the lift had stalled and we would have to stand by while engineers were called and could fix the problem. It took over an hour for them to get the lift working again. We chatted away happily while we waited for the engineers. Although Tiffany, who was still wearing Freddo's leather jacket that she'd borrowed for the show (that's the level of wardrobe and styling we had) didn't say much other than to ask at one point why the lift smelled so much of meat. Because it was the service lift, all the restaurants used it to bring their burgers and sausages up to the top floor and the whole thing did rather whiff of processed pork products. Such is the glamour of a young pop star's life, and her plugger's.

The lift eventually got working again and we spilled out, grateful for the relatively fresh air of the shopping centre. Tiffany, an absolute professional, delivered a thrilling set for the thousands of fans who by then had waited so long to see her. She didn't seem fazed by any of it. Luckily she had already experienced that level of hysteria in America and she was very cool about the crowds. But I hadn't seen anything on that scale before, it amazed me. And then along came Take That.

12

Time Can Do So Much

'What have you come dressed as today? A pirate?'

Simon Cowell is on top form this morning. Just because I'm wearing a stripey top (from Gap, with my new chinos. Loving this preppy look that's in at the moment). The cheek. He has some brilliant lines, this man. 'Do you mind, the grown-ups are talking,' he says to anyone and everyone. Always winks at me when he says that as well, I've noticed. Not in a suggestive way, more to let me know it's not for real, a 'we're in it together' kind of thing.

Very funny man, Simon Cowell. And very good-looking, it cannot be denied. He goes around with his packet of Kool menthol cigarettes tucked up into his T-shirt sleeve. They never fall out because the T-shirt is always so tight. And you know what? It works. Only Simon can get away with something like that.

'Have you got a minute, Chappers?' he asks. He calls me to his department, A&R, below.

'Always for you, Simon.'

We sit down on the grey sofa in his office. Charcoal-grey sofas seem to be very popular these days. They're everywhere. Jeremy's got a couple of them in his office as well. There are a pair of big fake plants on either side of us, with dust on the leaves. And a selection of the week's music press – NME, Music Week, Kerrang! – is arranged on the little coffee table in a fan shape. Simon's had a chat this morning, he says, with Denise Beighton. She works downstairs in sales. I love Denise, she's from Birmingham and has the best accent, it's brilliant. She and another colleague, Richard Perry, are both Brummies and we all tease them relentlessly. Denise and Simon are great mates. Simon is one of those men who gets on well with women, has a lot of female friends. There's no hidden agenda with Simon, none of the cat-and-mouse stuff. He's always got a very glamorous girlfriend too, so at work things are very straightforward with Simon, even if he does wear those high-waisted jeans. He and Denise have had a chat this morning and, apparently, she's tipped him the wink about Soldier, Soldier.

'Wait a minute. Soldier, Soldier? As in the drama on telly? My bestie Krista loves that.'

'Everyone loves that programme. And their mum.'

Denise has told him that after last night's episode, the phones are ringing off the hook, the record shops are all calling up asking if there is a single coming out. They say people have been asking in the shops all morning. The two main characters, played by loveable rogues, Robson Green and Jerome Flynn, did a rendition of 'Unchained Melody' by the Righteous Brothers and apparently it was very good. It always surprises people when their favourite actor turns out to have a good voice, but the truth is a lot of them have spent years at stage school or treading the boards and are brilliant all-round performers.

'What single?' I ask. It hasn't come up in any meetings recently. I didn't know they were doing a single.

'Exactly,' says Simon.

I don't watch *Soldier, Soldier*. I don't watch much normal television to be honest. I watch the programmes I need to watch for work. *The Tube* was a favourite and there's a great new show with Mark Radcliffe and Jo Whiley, *The White Room*. *The Word*, and *Top of the Pops* of course. Compulsory. I've been watching that ever since I can remember. I do like *ER*, the hospital drama with George Clooney. It's nice to come home and flop on my sofa and watch that on Channel 4 if I can catch it. Sometimes I'll even remember to record it. But I don't seem to have much time for television, which is ironic as that's my job, and my passion. I always seem to be home so late.

I've missed the whole *Soldier, Soldier* fever. This drama has gripped the nation. They're saying it's a really accurate portrayal of modern military life and I know plenty of people love it. Simon says the viewing figures are staggering – 16 million people watched it last night.

'This could be enormous, Nicki,' he says. I believe him. Those puppets he signed, Zig and Zag? Their debut single reached number 5 in the UK charts not so long ago, number 4 in Ireland. The man knows a hit when he sees one and he is always first off the mark. Once he's had an idea he doesn't hang around, he makes it happen. I have a lot of respect for that kind of attitude. Neither does he care if people laugh at him. Doesn't care a jot. That's actually a very powerful position to be in. I'm not a music snob either, I love my pop and a bit of house and I've always enjoyed working with the fictional characters as much as real ones. I did some work on *The Simpsons* years ago at MCA, remember 'Do The Bartman'? It was a blast. So we see each other, Simon Cowell and me. I trust Simon's judgement and he knows I get the job done. I'm definitely not laughing at him.

So Robson and Jerome it is. There's just one problem, he says. 'They don't want to do a single.'

I've never come across anyone who doesn't want to do a single! The artists I work with are usually desperate for a number 1 hit. So this is a new perspective. Simon's been doing everything he can to get hold of them. Apparently he's even called Robson's mum, which didn't go down well at all. Poor Mrs Green. I know he'll win them over eventually though. It's what he does.

I go home later that evening and switch on the television.

Mousing around

Adamski & I – a *killer* team!

Spiky? Not at all. Three beards . . . ZZ Top, the nicest guys even first thing in the morning

My boys! Taking That to TV and around
the world . . . Elstree, Venice & Tokyo

My RCA Gang and three friends for life – L-R Permy Chappers, Miller, Tigger, Rich$, DC, Shacky & Nick G

Shacky with his long hair again at a BMG Conference

The love of my life – but with short hair!

The start of it all in front of the camera: Nasty Nigel and lovely Paul Adam at *Popstars* auditions

'I'll have a Nicki Chapman, please' – the haircut at the National TV Awards

Hear'Say – proving they could stand the heat (in the kitchen!)

How high can they go? All the way with Denise van Outen in a hot-air balloon

A sixth member? I'll be Old Spice then . . .

With the judges and the winner (Will)
and the runner-up (Gareth)

Far from idle – the hosts that made TV history. And we still have that logo board in our loft!

Engaging with the King and the King Maker – (then) HRH Prince Charles and Simon Fuller

One of a kind – S Club 7 with their first #1 single award

And here we are!

Soldier, Soldier isn't on tonight but there are plenty of other dramas. One about a lifeboat crew, and a period drama of some kind. It has got me thinking, this whole thing. It's an interesting moment, in terms of my work. The acts have always come from the ground up, from the pubs and clubs. I've always seen television as something I need to make work for my artists, a tool to help them build their profiles and make fans aware of what they're doing, to help them achieve success, or at least maintain it. Now television is turning the tables, saying 'Here you go, here are some future stars. What are you going to do with them?'

What if Robson and Jerome is just the start? What will this job look like in the future, when the talent starts to cross over like this? Sure, we've had all the *Neighbours* cast releasing tracks with Stock Aitken and Waterman. But this is different, it's being driven by the viewers. It's interesting. I flick through the channels lazily for a bit, seeing if there are any more handsome actors on tonight who look like they can hold a tune. If only George Clooney would do a little crooning number on *ER*, I'd buy it.

A new health club has opened on the Upper Richmond Road, and I have signed up. It's a bit more upmarket than the local leisure centre, it has a pool and a steam room, and you can watch television in the gym. They have some great classes as well. Step aerobics, where you have to go up and down on a step and do all sorts of moves around it. I try to go before work as it gets me feeling ready for the day and I can have a good think about what I need to do. I'll go to step tomorrow and think about Robson and Jerome.

The next morning at step, while doing a move called a 'round the world', I conclude that *Surprise, Surprise!* is the perfect show for these two. It's the same ITV audience as *Soldier, Soldier* and the viewing numbers on a Sunday night are huge – 10, 12 million. Cilla Black, the host, has successfully straddled a career in music and television, and is an all-round entertainer, so it feels more appropriate than *Wogan* for Robson and Jerome. A lovely lady called Isobel Hutton is the producer. I've already had Kylie on there with her and we get along. I think she'll like the soldier boys a lot.

While I've been leaping up and down, not exactly Jane Fonda but giving it my best, Simon has somehow managed to persuade Robson and Jerome that a quick single won't do anyone any harm. I say, somehow, I hear he has offered them a huge amount of money to do it. I won't ask how much. Apparently they've refused to do *Top of the Pops* already and Simon's told them they don't have to. That's obviously not true. They absolutely have to do *Top of the Pops*. Thanks for that, Simon.

Although they're resistant I know this pair aren't being deliberately difficult. Because they're actors it's a big leap for them to suddenly find themselves in the charts, as pop stars. It's probably a bit uncomfortable for them, because it's not how they see themselves. It would be foolish of me to underestimate that reticence; it needs careful handling. Getting them to do children's television will be interesting!

Although I did manage to get ZZ Top on *What's Up Doc?* recently. If I can persuade those three old rockers to do a kids' television show talking to two wolf puppets called Bro and Bro, I reckon I can get Robson and Jerome on there.

I chuckle every time I think about that experience with ZZ Top. Billy, Dusty and Frank were over here in the UK to promote their single, 'Pincushion'. They're a world-renowned band; they've been around for decades, played every festival, travelled the world. They're used to staying in five-star hotels, taking limos everywhere. Me? I took them to a Travelodge just outside Maidstone in Kent, not far from where my dad lives. There wasn't anywhere else close enough to the television studio and we had to make an early start on the Saturday morning. So I drove them down with Shacky, who is their product manager, on Friday night and we all checked in to the Travelodge.

I hadn't had a lot of time to plan this, it had come in at the last minute. I realised we now had a whole evening ahead of us with ZZ Top to entertain, just off the M25 in Kent. I could see them thinking 'Where the hell are we and who is this woman?'

I had one hope, and that was my dad. We weren't far from where he lives so I called him up and asked casually:

'Dad, what can I do with ZZ Top?'

'Oh blimey. What do you mean?'

'Well, I'm staying just down the road from you and I need to entertain ZZ Top for the night. The hotel is too boring. What can we do?'

'I know what you can do, Nic. Take them to the Little Gem. It's one of the oldest pubs in England. It's just up the road. It'll take you ten minutes to get there. It's absolutely tiny, twelfth century. It will blow their minds.'

So that's what we did. Dad was right about the pub, it was minute! ZZ Top loved it because it was so old, older than America and full of character and charm. No security, no entourage, just ZZ Top, Shacky and I. They are one of the world's most instantly recognisable bands so everybody in the pub did a double-take as soon as we walked in. All the regulars wanted to buy them a drink. The whole village turned up. People brought their beer mats to get them signed. The guys loved it, kept banging their heads because the beams are so low in there. Then of course when the landlord called time at 11 p.m., no one moved. We stayed there until well into the small hours and I had a real job getting them back to the hotel.

The next morning, everybody was a little bit green around the gills and the heads were still banging, but for a slightly different reason. Billy told me it was one of the most fun promos they'd ever done. Forget five-star restaurants and private jets, jam them into a tiny twelfth-century pub in Kent and buy them a round or five. It's a winner.

13

Back For Good

It's late afternoon and everyone's desk lights are coming on, because it's the time of year when it gets dark too early. The sandwich man came round this morning and I bought myself a KitKat that I have so far managed to resist, but it's living on borrowed time. Shall I eat it now or after I've made this call? That sandwich man will be the death of me. He comes in every morning with his big basket of sandwiches and chocolate bars, along with the odd bruised apple that no one ever wants. Every day I tell myself I'm not having anything and then he turns up with fresh ciabatta rolls, and I always give in and buy one. It's very clever marketing, really. You have to be quick though. If you're on the phone or haven't heard him you end up with the squashed one at the bottom, with the coleslaw all running out of the cling-film wrapper.

I head into the kitchen to make a coffee before I make the call. I'm not looking forward to this conversation. I'm flagging and it will be stressful. The Take That boys are in the midst of a promo trip to Japan and I need to talk to Nigel about getting them home for a performance on *Top of the Pops*. Shacky comes in; he always appears for a chat when I make a coffee. He says he's going to steal my KitKat if I leave it out on my desk much longer. Then he asks if I'm OK and I explain about Nigel and Take That not coming back for *Top of the Pops*.

Nigel is such a character, wonderfully outrageous at times. Strong, opinionated and occasionally damn stubborn. He was teasing me the other day that my necklace looks like a cock ring. It's a black leather string with a thick silver hoop around it and he was going 'Nicki, look, it's a cock ring! What are you doing with a cock ring around your neck you naughty girl!' I didn't even know there was such a thing as a cock ring, had no idea what you would do with one, and he had to explain it to me. Well, let's just say now I do know, and it's all thanks to Nigel.

So we're solid, Nigel and I. But he's always fighting with the label, and occasionally the boys. There's always something he doesn't like or something RCA is asking for that he doesn't agree with. He can be quite contrary when he wants to be. They say black and he says white. But he likes me. And so, because we're friends, I have become the conduit between Nigel and the label. It all comes through me. It's great to have his trust but it also means I have to get involved in all sorts of things that I don't necessarily want to be involved in. Or indeed, that I know nothing about.

Today he's refusing to fly the band back from Japan for *Top of the Pops* on Thursday. He's saying the boys are exhausted, which I'm sure is true.

'If anyone can get them back, it's you,' says Shacky as we head back into the office. I roll my eyes at him in a way that says 'easy for you to say' and sit down at my desk. The KitKat will have to wait.

I dial Nigel's number. 'Nigel? Hello? It's Nic.

'Please Nigel. Just let them do this one performance of "Relight My Fire" for *Top of the Pops*.'

He says on the other end: 'They've got jet lag, darling, they've been working non-stop. For once I'm going to say no, we're not doing it.'

Jeremy, my Managing Director, John Preston, the Chairman of RCA, and Hugh Goldsmith, the Marketing Director, have told me in no uncertain terms that the boys need to appear on *Top of the Pops* this week. It's an unspoken rule with artists that they need to make themselves available for promotion. In the UK, there is no promotion more vital, and directly responsible for sales, than *Top of the Pops*. It's the biggest and best thing we have, so to hear Nigel saying they're not flying back for it is frustrating to say the least. That said, I know only too well how tiring their schedule is, and why the thought of a transatlantic flight and a performance on *Top of the Pops* might not be very appealing to them right now.

'Nigel, what can I do for you? What will it take? I can hire a private plane, to make the journey as smooth as possible. Would that help?'

'No, Nicki darling, they're just too tired. A private plane doesn't make any difference.'

There's a receipt on my desk, underneath the KitKat, for the watch I bought recently. It is the most expensive thing I've ever bought, apart from my flat. I got it at Harrods, a total guilty pleasure that I am still feeling a bit naughty about. But it gives me an idea.

'I'll buy them all fabulous watches. How about that? From Harrods.'

I don't know what I'm saying, I am grasping at straws here. I'm just desperate to get them to come back.

'What kind of watches?' Ooh, he's biting.

'You have to come back and do *Top of the Pops* and I'll show you what watches I've bought. They'll be amazing, rest assured.'

After a long silence he sighs. 'All right, you win. We'll come back. For you.'

Phew. That's sorted. Now I just need to tell Jeremy I've promised all the members of Take That some very expensive watches. He did say I had to get them back at any cost. Not sure he meant this cost, but never mind.

A few days later and I'm in the dressing room with them

at Elstree after filming's finished. Everyone is in good spirits, although Robbie seems a little quiet. It looked to me a bit like he was positioning himself very slightly apart from the rest of them tonight. It was almost like he was performing by himself and they were the backing singers. I'm not sure anyone else noticed, but I'm so familiar with the way they all are together, I can tell something is different with him. At least he's not disappeared with someone from *EastEnders* tonight.

'Oh wow, Nicki! What are these for? They're amazing. Thank you so, so much. You didn't need to do that.' They're all hugging me and gawping in delighted shock at their beautiful new Tag Heuer diving watches, which I have to say are extremely nice, and gobsmackingly expensive. Nigel's face is a picture when I produce an extra one for him. The boys don't seem to know anything about the watch situation or not coming home for *Top of the Pops*. They have no idea why they are being given these ostentatious gifts, or that I have had to bribe Nigel with bling to get them here. The penny drops – it was Nigel who didn't want them to fly back. I look at him and he gives me a look back that says 'So sue me.' I'm rolling my eyes at him in return but I do get it. He is trying to protect them, to look after their health, give them some space to breathe. They are all clearly tired, and being together round the clock is starting to take its toll on them. I can feel the discontent just under the surface.

They're such a mixed bag of personalities, all with their

own different strengths. I'm closest to Gary. We've become friends ever since he started coming down to London by himself to write. Having composed and written from an early age, he's the one who writes the bulk of the songs so he's here in the studio, working with other writers and producers. We both love going out and he says, 'Eh Nicki C, do you fancy taking me out for dinner later?' I'm always happy to join him. We go to My Old Dutch, a traditional pancake restaurant on the King's Road, near his hotel, La Reserve, in Chelsea. They serve the pancakes on huge blue and white plates, and they aren't just ordinary pancakes. You can have any filling you want in them. I always go for the sweet: banana, vanilla ice cream and chocolate sauce. GB usually goes for the savoury option, he likes a ham and cheese. We get on well; he's a very thoughtful, reflective person, and I've got so much time for him. Once when we were in Newcastle for a show, he played me a song that he wrote years ago when he was a teenager, called 'Why Can't I Wake Up With You?' It was just us in the hotel bar, him on a white piano, and all the reception staff behind us watching with their mouths open. He wanted to know what I thought of it. That was a real star-spangled moment: me and GB in the hotel bar, him playing a new song for me. He gave me a cassette of it the next day and I've still got it at home. I'm keeping that one for ever.

Robbie too is very special, but I think of him as more like a naughty younger brother who I've got to try and keep under control. I'm very fond of him though. He came out shopping with Shelley and me once. We took him down the King's Road to buy new clothes. This was not very long ago, when they weren't so easily recognised and tracked everywhere by teenage girls, who are like bloodhounds. I could tell he loved being out and about without the rest of them, without the security drawing attention to him. I think he feels his talent doesn't have the space to shine sometimes. He loves to try his hand at writing and putting together the raps, but it's probably not enough. Plus, his image outside the band is starting to be a problem. That whole Glastonbury debacle, dyeing his hair and partying with the Gallaghers while clearly off his face, didn't go down well at all with the label. I felt awful because we'd been at a charity lunch earlier that day and I helped him smuggle four bottles of champagne out to take to the festival. I'll keep that one to myself. God knows what else he had in his pockets.

And of course there was the MTV Europe Awards in Berlin. It still gives me the shivers thinking about it. I thought for a moment that we might have lost him. The ceremony was taking place by the Brandenburg Gate; the wall had come down only a few years before and the show was going to go out, live, to the whole of Europe and America. Take That have a huge following in Germany; we've been to the country a few times now, and the crowds were enormous. Tonight everyone you could think of – Prince, Bjork, George Michael – was playing. It was a big deal and, for the boys, one of the biggest 'moments' so far.

We were all there the day before for rehearsals and afterwards we went for a few drinks, as you do. It carried on a little longer than usual, everyone was in high spirits and buzzing from seeing so many other stars around. After a while most of the boys left and went to bed, so it ended up just Robbie, Michael Hutchence, Helena Christensen, Naomi Campbell and a whole group of others in the hotel bar. Oh, and me. I was enjoying myself, I don't often get to hang out with supermodels, but I was also aware I had to keep an eye on Robbie. He was playing with the grown-ups, and they were partying hard. I knew some of them were probably doing God knows what, as they were all wired while I was getting more and more sleepy. By 4 a.m. I said to Robbie: 'I'm going to bed, Rob.'

He said: 'No, no, no, Nicki, don't leave, don't leave, don't leave.' He was slurring his words and his eyes were all over the place.

I said to our security guy as I left: 'I've had enough. We've got a big day tomorrow. Please just get him to bed.'

The next morning I went down to join the boys at rehearsals. No Robbie, and no one knew where he was. Nigel appeared, he'd been hammering on Robbie's door. 'I can't find him. He's not answering the phone in his room, not opening the door.' The security guys said they saw him into his room, so he had to be in there. The reasons why he might not be answering were flashing through my mind.

After some more fruitless hammering, I went down to

reception and got a spare key. Opening the door, the sight that greeted me was not pretty. Robbie was flat on his back, out like a light, still fully dressed, a sheen of sweat all over him. Cigarette ends everywhere, and I hate to think what else was lying around. He also reeked of booze. This was the biggest TV show of their lives – millions and millions of people, the whole of Europe and America. And this boy was out for the count. I checked he was breathing. He was, praise be! It's easy to pass this kind of thing off as rock'n'roll, but he was so young and I kept imagining what I'd have to tell everyone if he had overdosed. I couldn't bear to think about it. Even a less terrible outcome – maybe he'd passed out and wouldn't be able to perform – could have potentially ruined the whole event, in front of the whole world.

I left Nigel in Robbie's room trying to wake him up and ran downstairs to reception again, trying to find a first-aider or a doctor. By some incredible stroke of luck, Prince's personal physician happened to be in the hotel lobby, dressed head to toe in hospital whites. It was almost as if he was going to burst into a comedy routine or something; he couldn't have been dressed more like a doctor if he had tried. That is, apart from the white wellies he was wearing. On an already surreal morning, this vision of a man only seemed to confirm that working in this business is sometimes like living in an alternative universe. He was German and didn't speak any English, while I don't speak any German, but somehow he seemed to know what I needed and after

I offered him some money he followed me upstairs into Robbie's room.

The doctor – I mean who even knows if he really was a doctor – took a big needle out of his bag and gave Robbie an injection. I didn't ask what it was, but I hoped it was vitamins or something good. Frankly I didn't want to know. After a few terrifying moments, Robbie began to stir. He started smacking his lips because his mouth was so dry. His eyes surveyed the room and when they eventually met mine he said: 'Right, up we get.'

The guy is a pure showman. He gave one of the most phenomenal performances of his life. Afterwards, I told him he'd given me a scare and he said: 'I'd never let you down, Nicki C.'

Later on everyone was joking about it and ribbing him. All I could think was how I'd felt when I first saw him, when I opened that door and saw his motionless body. There is high jinks and all of that, I've always known the boys occasion- ally enjoy a few a special rollies after a gig. But this wasn't funny. I had to ask myself if I had been irresponsible, leaving him there when I knew what was happening. It was a lesson learned for me, that artists have to be accountable for their own actions. Robbie was – is – young and impressionable, only twenty years of age, and I felt angry with the people I'd left him with in that hotel bar, especially Michael, who I have met a few times now. And of course I was livid with Robbie himself. But ultimately it's down to him, isn't it?

Management at RCA aren't happy; there are mutterings about his behaviour. They keep reminding him he's supposed to be in a pop band, he's not meant to be a solo artist or a rock star. But that's just who he is. I always say you can't manufacture talent or force it in a direction it doesn't want to take. Robbie's a born performer who has to find his path. He's discovering who he is and you can't make him be someone he's not. Still, they've all grown up together in many ways. It's hard to imagine things changing.

14

Surprise, Surprise!

As predicted, Robson and Jerome's single went straight in at number 1 and has not moved from the top spot for some time. The sales figures for 'Unchained Melody' are unbelievable. They've sold something like 1.5 million copies so far and it's showing no sign of slowing down. That series of *Soldier, Soldier* has ended and people are holding on to it for dear life with this song. It's already on track to be the biggest single of the year. Rumour has it Simon Cowell has bought Denise Beighton a Rolex to thank her for the tip-off.

Of course, the boys eventually gave in on the television appearance issue and agreed to do it. The wonderful Isobel Hutton at *Surprise, Surprise!* had them on as I'd hoped she would. They have been on *Top of the Pops* a couple of times now, too, though they still don't like it. They do it with their tongues in their cheeks, I think that's the best way to describe how they deal with it. Being pop stars just isn't where they've ever seen themselves. I know they've also given a huge amount of their royalties to Greenpeace, which makes you love them even more.

This evening is their third time on *Top of the Pops* and they've both been winding me up since we arrived for rehearsal, saying, 'You know we were never meant to do this show, Nicki. Why are we here? We're actors, darling, not pop stars.' A bit of light teasing really, to remind me that they're kind of here against their will, but in a good way.

I left them in make-up earlier and went to talk to the string quartet I've got set up for the other mini 'riser' stage. Robson and Jerome will be miming tonight, not because they can't sing but because it's much better for the sound quality of the show when the artist mimes. People often don't seem to realise this; they think artists mime because they can't sing. In fact it is very hard to get a clean sound when the acoustics in a studio may not be ideal. You may not have the sound engineer you need, there can be timing constraints or the room is full of screaming fans and you can't hear a bloody thing. It's often better just to play the track and have the artist mime. The string quartet on their riser are also miming; they're there to keep the performance interesting.

Now I've come back to the dressing room to give the

boys something to eat before the show. It is always helpful
to have a snack or a light meal available for the artists, as it
will usually be quite late by the time they get out of here.
Not everyone wants to eat before they go on, but these two
never turn down a meal. They're soldiers, after all.

I push open the door with my back because I've got a
big silver foil tray full of sandwiches in one hand and my
new Mulberry Filofax (a treat to self) and enormous mobile
phone in the other. When I turn round I see the room is
empty, apart from the make-up assistant who is packing up
her kit.

'What the hell? Where are they?' There isn't anywhere
else on-site that I would expect them to be at this point
before the show, so this empty scene is not something my
mind is prepared to process. I quickly scan the room. The
dressing room has its own shower room and the door is
open, but I can see they're not in there.

'Really sorry, Nicki,' she says, 'they just left a minute ago.
Walked out.'

'What do you mean?' I can feel my pulse start racing. I've
been here before with Bobby Brown and it was over a chuff-
ing burger. I don't want to repeat that episode.

'They've just left. They said they didn't want to do it. Said
they were too tired, fed up and they just left.'

Oh my God. This cannot be happening.

I'm still holding the tray of sandwiches. There's a few
veggie rolls that I've had made especially for Jerome. 'Well,

have they had anything to eat?' I don't know why I'm asking her but it feels important. I've been in enough dressing rooms with enough artists by now to know that food doesn't solve everything, but if you can take being hungry off the list of potential problems, it's a start. Have I taken too long with the sandwiches? Have they left in a fit of hanger? Not exactly rock'n'roll, I know, but hey, priorities.

'I've got loads of food here for them. Do you know if they had anything to eat?' The assistant is looking at me like I'm mad. Why would she know if they've had anything to eat? And why am I so obsessed with them eating?

'I've got all these sandwiches,' I say, to drive home my disappointment. I think she thinks I'm going to cry. She looks terrified.

And then. 'Surprise, surprise!'

Jerome bursts out of the wardrobe in the corner, swiftly followed by Robson, the pair of them puce in the face from stifling their laughter in that tiny wardrobe. It's a wonder it didn't break open.

Very funny, boys. I'm pretty sure this would have been Robson's idea, not Jerome's. Robson is the naughty, playful one with the twinkle in his eye. Jerome is more considered, he's the serious one who thinks everything through. Still, if they're having fun I'm happy, it means everything is OK. I'm glad I didn't say anything unpleasant about them. Imagine if I'd blown my top and said: 'What the fuck do they think they're playing at?'

My mind flicks back to a moment, in the studio next door, a few years ago. I was inexperienced but well-meaning. I'd confirmed that an artist would appear on a certain Saturday-morning television show, but unbeknown to me their manager had agreed to put them on the competitor show on the other channel, something to do with a deal involving another of his acts. All behind my back. Management don't usually book television appearances, so I had no way of knowing what he'd arranged. When he found out his deal was scuppered he was furious. He walked straight up to me, pushed me against the wall, got me by the throat and told me never to do anything without his say-so again. I should have kicked him in the balls, it's something I regret not doing. But he was very strong and far bigger than me. And it worked. I've never done anything like that again with any of his artists.

I glance at the make-up girl, who looks relieved the joke is well and truly over. Poor thing. *Top of the Pops* will proceed. At least I didn't get her by the throat. It's another smasher of a show for the boys; they've got a 1940s-style microphone and they're wearing their old-timey suits and both look so handsome. Women (and men) of all ages across the nation are in love with them. There's already been talk about them releasing another single, and an album. It would be more covers of heartbreak classics, like 'Unchained Melody'. I think there is plenty of mileage in their whole concept and it couldn't happen to two nicer fellows. I just hope they can come to terms with being singers. I know they both take their careers as actors very seriously.

I don't hang around tonight as I want to get home to my flat and get a good night's sleep. Simon Fuller is coming in to the office tomorrow with this new girl band he wants me to see. With Robbie having left Take That not so long ago, there's certainly a five-piece gap in my roster. Although I'm still working with the boys of course – they're still Take That. I was worried they wouldn't feel like Take That when Robbie went but they really do. Nigel did always say he had five of them in case one left.

When I get home my friend Andrea (not the Andrea I was at college with; I seem to know a few Andreas) is there on the sofa bed in the living room. She's split up with her boyfriend and is staying with me for a while. It's nice to see her smiling face when I get home. We have a nightcap and I tell her about Robson and Jerome playing that joke on me. She loves hearing about my work, she can't believe some of the stories. Then she asks me how Greg is. She's noticed I don't see much of him in the week. Is everything OK? She's right, we don't see much of each other at all, and he only lives down the road. I've been so busy and having such a good time at work, I haven't really noticed. The truth is he and I aren't going anywhere.

I take off my make-up and brush my hair in my little bathroom in the eaves. It's not an avocado bathroom suite, but it's kind of beige and probably not what I would have chosen, but it was there already when I bought the flat and it works for now. As I get under the covers, I notice my dried flower wreath has lost its perfume, and as sleep creeps up on me I am wondering whether I should get a new one or find something different to put in its place.

15

Love Letters Straight From Your Heart

I bump into Shacky as I walk into reception this morning. It's been more than a month since I saw him and read his letter. It doesn't feel weird or embarrassing though. It's good to see him.

The run-up to Christmas last year was mayhem. Robson and Jerome's album was number 1 so everyone wanted them on their Christmas specials, and Take That. It was non-stop for me. I didn't have a day off at all, didn't get a break. I realised I'd worked forty weekends out of fifty-two in the year. January is always quiet so Nick said I should take the month off. A whole month to myself. I wasn't sure what I would do with it at first. Then I remembered I was meant to be moving to Australia. It turns out I am terrible at moving to Australia, but that doesn't mean I can't visit. Nick said go, so I went. I stayed with Aunty Liz and Uncle Bob and my cousins. I got some much-needed sunshine, caught up with my Aussie friends, drank too much West Coast Cooler, saw plenty of live bands and stocked up on Tim Tam biscuits.

I had a few drinks after work with everyone before I left and towards the end of the evening Shacky handed me a letter, sealed in an envelope. He said: 'Don't open this until you're on the plane.'

'What is it? What does it say?'

'Just open it on the plane.' And that was it. He went home. I said my goodbyes to everyone and left. I very nearly opened it later that night, and in fact quite a few times before I got to the airport. I managed to resist until I was on the tarmac, waiting to board. I figured that was as good as being on the plane.

I didn't know what to expect, although I had an idea. We've become close, that's for sure. We don't always work together but we are part of a tight team. There's him and me, my boss Nick, Narrinder and the brilliant Brummie Richard Perry, who is always trying to matchmake Shacky and me. And we have a new girl in the department, Carys, she's a radio plugger, and my assistant, Tam. We all spend a lot of time together, every day really. We're like a little family. Shacky and I are always laughing and taking the mick, and I know he's got my back. Talk about opposites!

I'm pop and he's rock. But that doesn't seem to get in the way of our connection.

The letter was so heartfelt and open. He said he wanted to tell me when I had time to think. That he felt certain I am the one for him and he wants us to be together. Would I think about it while I'm away?

It's the most romantic thing anyone has ever done for me. A handwritten love letter like that. I do feel there is something there. But me, with a rocker? A Leeds United fan in a leather jacket? It seems so unlikely. Besides which, Greg and I are still hanging on by a thread and the thought of another relationship with someone I work with seems unimaginable right now.

I haven't replied yet, or even spoken to him since I got back. I owe him some kind of reply but I honestly don't know what I want to say. And now here we are in reception, as though no letter has ever changed hands. We both break into big grins and after some initial chat I find we are talking about work again, which feels safe and familiar. I do value his opinion, I'll always check in with him on things. Today I need to get to work on Kylie and M People, who are both on Deconstruction, the dance label on the third floor. Shacky has worked with Republica and knows the other Deconstruction acts, people like Black Box and Felix, so he's always good for the inside track on everything that's going on down there.

They're a cool bunch at Deconstruction. I always see

them trickling in late on Mondays with their sunglasses on. I don't know how they do it. If we go out after work we sometimes end up in Le Fez, the local club here in Putney (it has a light-up dance floor). And I love a night out in town at the Atlantic, Ministry of Sound or the new Conran place in Soho, Mezzo – they have some great live music there. People steal the ashtrays because they're so nice. But some of the Deconstruction guys and gals are out all weekend clubbing and taking Lord knows what. I don't have a problem with people doing whatever they like, and goodness knows I do get the opportunity, but drugs aren't for me. I always say I'd rather have a cup of tea. Plus I work most weekends. It's just the way it is when your job is in television promotion. Like Jeremy said, if you want a normal job, go work in a bank. I'm not complaining, but there's just no way I could be up all night taking pills like a lot of them do.

So I don't consider myself to be one of the cool set, although I do love some of the dance acts. With signings like Kylie and M People they are really moving into a more mainstream area and that's my happy place.

'Let me know how it goes,' Shacky says after I've picked his brains and he has teased me ruthlessly about the green culottes I'm wearing today, 'Is it trousers or is it a dress? Is it a trouser-dress? Dress-trousers?' and I have pretended to punch him in the face.

'I shall do that!'

I make my way up to my desk. I need to talk to Suzi Aplin,

the producer at *TFI Friday*, about Kylie going on the show. People always want to know about Kylie: what's she like, what she says. She's one of those artists that everyone loves. I never watched much of *Neighbours*, the Aussie soap she rose to fame in, as I was always at work when it was on. But my mum loved it, and plenty of people I know watched it when they were students – sometimes twice a day, the same episode! People were so invested in that show, I reckon some of them could answer specialist questions on *Mastermind* about it. Quite a few acts came out of *Neighbours*, and the other Aussie soap *Home and Away*, but few of them have the star quality of Kylie.

Perhaps because she was a child actor, she's a true professional to work with, a real joy. Very likeable and with a wicked sense of humour. I first met her when she came in to the label with her manager Terry Blamey. He's another Aussie and he is always with Kylie, at every show and every meeting. A very dedicated man and a reassuring presence for her, I'm sure, as he's been with Kylie and her sister Dannii from the start. In such a fickle business that kind of solidarity is golden. Kylie was so friendly and warm, remembered everyone's names. She had on a pair of quite loose black jeans and a white cropped T-shirt with a ripped denim waistcoat over the top and her hair down, all loose and curly. I instantly wanted to wear everything she had on, but she is so tiny, she can carry anything off. And she can change her look so easily, like a chameleon. It's the same with her sound.

She's with Deconstruction now as she's moving into a more dance-led space with her music. Her most recent single, 'Confide in Me', went down a storm with the critics and gave her some much-needed music cred after the sugar-pop of the Stock Aitken and Waterman years.

I had her on *Surprise, Surprise!* and *Eurotrash* with 'Confide in Me' and got to know her while covering those shows. Although she's not one to gossip, she's very private. She often has her best friend come along with her, which is a pretty wise move. She's been a performer for years, so she has probably learned how to manage and balance her private life and her career – although I did see a small chink in the armour when we were filming *Eurotrash* in Paris. Jean Paul Gaultier asked a question about her former romance with Michael Hutchence and she answered it extremely well, but when we came off the set she was in tears. A chink in the armour. I can't imagine how distressing it must be when certain aspects of your private life are broadcast to millions of people. Sometimes I think it must be very lonely being a performer, all those long journeys and time away from the people you love.

I'm a massive fan of Kylie's, but the only complaint I have is that she's often not here. She's so busy, and an international star, so I am always in a long queue of people vying for her time. She was filming the *Street Fighter* movie with Jean-Claude Van Damme for months and is often back in Australia where her family is and where she's had a string of number 1s. It's frustrating because I know I can sell Kylie's records when she's here, and I can get her on British television. She has a new single coming out soon and she's going to be around for a bit, so I'm trying to set up a gig with Chris Evans.

'Hi Suzi, how are you doing? Have you got a minute to catch up on Kylie?'

'Oh, OK. Um, sure Nicki, we can do that.'

She sounds a bit strange, as though she's surprised I'm calling.

'Is it not a good time?'

'No, it's not that, Nicki. Look, I'll be honest. Spanner has already called me about this. He said he was looking after Kylie's promo so I've been dealing with him on this one.'

Spanner? Why does Spanner think he's handling Kylie's promo? I know Spanner vaguely; he used to work with a friend of Nick's, Neil Ferris, at an independent promotion company. Spanner is his nickname as he's always got a TV or radio presenter in his grip.

'Oh! How strange. Why would he say that? So sorry, Suze, let me find out what's going on.'

I'm straight up to see Nick in his office. He's typing something, staring intently at his screen. I launch straight in.

'Knock, knock. Why does Suzi Aplin at *TFI* think Spanner is now working Kylie's promo, please?'

He takes a deep breath and clicks out of whatever document he is in before even making eye contact with me. We are good friends, Nick and I, so I know something is awry, and that he's going to be straight.

'I've literally just heard myself. Deconstruction is going it alone. Doing its own thing with promo. You're to focus only on the main RCA roster.'

'Right. And this has just been announced, has it? No one thought to discuss it with me? Just the little old Head of Television?'

I've gone from nought to livid, to be honest. Not only have Kylie and a bunch of other Deconstruction acts, M People for one, just been wiped from my roster but no one has bothered to tell me. I was talking to Normski and the producers at *Dance Energy* about a raft of potential shows only last week. How can this be right?

'I told Jeremy you wouldn't be happy. He said it's not up for discussion. Plenty for you to be concentrating on at RCA, were his words.'

Wow. I don't swear often but I say a word I don't want to repeat and head back to my desk. Talk about insulting. What's the point in being the Head of Television if the top brass decide big things like this without even consulting me? I bet this was decided on that trip they all went on. All the men in management went on a skiing holiday recently. I'm furious.

It's lunchtime now and Simon Fuller is due in shortly with these girls. I'll have to come back to this. I write on a Post-it note and stick it on Nick's computer screen: 'Let's talk. Not happy.'

16

Losing My Mind

The door opens slightly and two young women on roller skates blast through it into the room. Three more women leap in behind them, wearing huge platform trainers and boots, a glittery human rainbow. Someone hits play on a ghetto blaster and they are off.

'So! Tell me what you want, what you really, really want.'

They are jumping all over the place. Two are on the chairs at the far end of the meeting room, one is doing an actual backflip in roller skates. It's a good job we moved the table back before this meeting. They are really going for it – great dancers, great sound. And they're all gorgeous but in different ways. This is brilliant.

The song is all about friendship and has an incredibly catchy pop hook. I know it will fly. Simon Fuller is grinning from ear to ear in the corner as the routine comes to an end with a word I have to say I've never heard before but works nevertheless.

'Ziga-zig-aaahhh.'

There's a moment of silence and then we burst out laughing. Hugh Goldsmith, our Marketing Director, and I stand up and applaud them, along with Simon. He's obviously seen this routine many times before but I can tell he's happy about how it went. It would take someone very miserable with a heart of stone not to have enjoyed that. They are an explosion of fun and because they all look so different to one another, it's impossible to take your eyes off them.

There's one with red hair and big boobs in shiny platform boots, and another more cutesy one with long blonde bunches in a little pink baby-doll dress, also wearing huge platform trainers. There's a gorgeous feisty one in a corset and huge hair, who you wouldn't mess with, and a cheeky gymnast-looking girl in a tracksuit. And at the back a quiet, elegant one in a little black dress, with the sleekest dark bob hairstyle I've ever seen. They all seem to be referencing a different pop or youth culture or style or something, but it's not textbook, they've got an energy of their own. They're definitely individuals but also working as a group. They are going to get a record deal, there's no doubt. The question right now is, who do they want to go with?

'Girls, I am stunned. You were unbelievable. What's the name of your group?'

'We're Spice!' they say in unison. They're all still a bit out of breath and obviously on a high. They say this with a twirl and do a few 'woo-hoos!'

Because of the news I've had this morning, I'm feeling slightly different in this situation to how I might normally do. I haven't told anyone yet but I know already that I am leaving RCA. I don't want to feel I'm not in control of my own destiny. Like they can just take a whole swathe of my work away without even consulting me. Maybe I'll set up on my own? I don't know. But I do know I'm not staying. Chappers needs to move on. So I feel a little bit more, shall we say, free in this room right now. I'm still employed by RCA so I need to be seen to do my job properly and get this act on board. But I also have the mental clarity of someone who has recently seen the light.

The girls are going around all the different record labels, deciding which one to go with. We're not meant to be interviewing them, they are interviewing me – us – in a way. Simon is staying back, letting them take the lead. Or maybe they're letting him tag along.

'What can you tell us about RCA?'

The redhead seems to be the spokeswoman. She asks me to tell them a bit about how we work. I give them the fairly standard rundown of how the company is structured, who would be working on them and what kind of vision RCA would have for them in terms of their television and radio promotions. As I'm speaking she keeps interjecting with contradictions:

'Well, we're not going on that' and 'We don't like that show' and 'We're not getting up at 4 a.m. to go on that!'

I always say there is a fine line between arrogance and confidence. I don't think she is being deliberately arrogant, but her confidence is certainly misplaced here in this moment, and because I've pretty much decided I'm leaving anyway I say:

'Do you know what, Geri. It is Geri, isn't it? Geri, you know, if we work together, and I sincerely hope that we do, but if we work together I want to give you a little bit of advice, if I may.'

They go quiet and I can see Simon's face in the corner of my eye. He can sense something is up with me, I know. He shifts his weight from one foot to the other.

'You girls are brilliant. Truly brilliant. You're really good at what you do. And so am I. So you do what *you're* good at, and I'll do what *I'm* good at, which happens to be breaking pop groups like you from nowhere into mainstream success, and we'll get along just fine. How does that sound?'

Without hesitation, they all chime in, pointing at me and high-fiving: 'We like that!' 'Love that, Nicki.' 'No messing. Love it.' 'You go, girl!'

I really like this bunch, they are mayhem but they are for real. One hundred per cent authentic and each one genuinely has something special. I'm reminded that true talent can't be manufactured. When you find yourself in its presence, it is always something to behold.

I wave them off and head back to my desk. Whatever happens, that was a damn good meeting. I feel like I need to talk to Shacky. Leaving RCA would mean leaving him, and the rest of the team. I scan the office to see if he's around.

Before I can locate him, Simon Fuller calls my mobile from reception.

'Told you, didn't I?'

'You did! They're great, Simon. What did they think of RCA?'

'They want to go with Virgin.'

'Oh. That's a shame. I felt we had a connection, you know. I'm quite surprised by that.'

'But they want to work with you, Nicki. They don't want to go with RCA. But they love you.'

17

Friendship Never Ends

It's about 9 p.m. and I'm stood shivering in what was once the reception of the old Midland Grand Hotel at St Pancras station, on London's Euston Road. If you listen carefully you can still hear the grandeur fading in here. It's been empty for years but was once a gorgeous Victorian-Gothic hotel. You can tell it would have been impressive – the staircase alone is enormous, like something from a Hollywood film. There are rumours this whole area is going to be renovated and there's going to be Europe's longest champagne bar next door. I could do with a champagne bar right now.

Instead, I'm clutching my travel mug of tea for warmth, watching the girls in hair and make-up. You can see everyone's breath it's so damn cold. Melanie C and Mel B are wearing tight crop tops and you can see their nipples are showing through. I wonder if we'll have problems with some of the international censors over those nipples. These are the things you have to think about on a music video shoot, honestly. The spooky Gothic ruined hotel is all ours and although I am sure my toes are about to fall off, I can't think of anywhere else I'd rather be.

We're here shooting the video for the Spice Girls' first single, 'Wannabe'. The idea behind the video is that it will be like a big house party (hence the night-time filming) full of eccentrics and stuffy elderly people, and the girls crash the party and cause mayhem as they tear through the place. Melanie C does a brilliant backflip on a dining table at one point. They've got Victoria sitting on a priest's lap, they're all stealing drinks and draping themselves over everyone. It's like a grown-up St Trinian's film, raucous and fun, and despite having heard the track, especially the intro, at least a million times already, I never tire of it. Geri went over on her ankle in some skyscraper shoes as she belted around the set, but there were no moans. The girls are just so great at going again and again and again. They never complain. Always bring the energy, even though I know they are exhausted. They are like Duracell bunnies, all of them.

They went out for dinner with Simon and Annie Lennox recently. Simon said Annie gave them some great advice about owning their image and how they look. She told them to let whoever they are really shine and be proud. Such great advice from a real icon. *Top of the Pops* magazine ran a front cover of them as different spices. They put their faces on actual spice jars, which I thought was hilarious. So they're all embracing their individual characteristics, shall we say.

There was actually an issue around their name. It turns out there is a US rapper called Spice so they became Spice Girls, although after some research it seems that might also be the name of a less than salubrious website on the World Wide Web. The web, or the internet as some people call it, is becoming something I have to consider now. Bands and artists are starting to get their own websites. We had a big talk about how to 'surf the web' a few months before I left RCA. Apparently it is going to be massive. I've only just about mastered opening a document on my new Apple iMac. The screen looks like a huge bubble with grey and strawberry pink casing.

Spice Girls is taken but The Spice Girls isn't, so I think I may buy thespicegirls.com for Simon and the girls instead, as no one has so far. They're officially the Spice Girls now. Small t on the 'the'. Not sure why, but hey! And here we are filming their first video. My favourite part is where they push past a couple of policemen and pile onto a big double-decker bus at the end, like they're just ordinary girls catching the night bus home. That's their appeal, they're relatable to young women everywhere.

I've been involved in video shoots with my artists before, of course. The iconic video with Take That for 'Back for Good' was the first one I was closely involved in. I spent the whole day tumble-drying their shirts because they were being pelted with water. Their wardrobe was vintage, they had big fur coats and hats on, so there were no spares or duplicates. If something got wet, which it all did, it had to be dried out in double quick time. The boys wore silk thermals because it was so cold and afterwards nobody wanted to keep them. So I scooped them up and gave them to Shelley to sell at her kids' school fair. Someone somewhere has got a nice piece of Take That memorabilia! What a video that was. One of their most legendary, I think, directed by a wonderful director, Vaughan Arnell. He'd done George Michael's video for 'Fastlove' this year as well. I didn't know it at the time but 'Back for Good' was the last video Take That did together before Robbie left. Ironic when you think about it. Sometimes when I watch it back I think I can see him looking discontented even then. He'd cropped most of his hair off and dyed what was left bright orange; it was a good job it was shot in black and white. But at RCA I wasn't always able to spend time on shoots like that. I wasn't as close to the creative process as I am now with the Spice Girls. And the visual side of things is only going to become more important for my artists. With all the new cable channels coming through via Sky and Virgin, the videos are almost as important as the song now. Michael and Janet Jackson's video for 'Scream' reportedly cost over $7 million to make. I do love that video, but don't suppose I'll be handling that kind of budget any time soon. It still only feels like yesterday that I was duping Kim Wilde's videos in the cupboard at MCA.

Now I'm at Brilliant! PR, I'm handling a smaller roster of artists and it means I'm more in charge of my own destiny. I get to decide who I want to work with. That's why I'm here in this big old hotel. I'm the co-director at the company and the Spice Girls are one of my acts. It's me, Nick Godwyn and our co-director, Neil Ferris. Just the three of us, doing PR and promotions. After RCA told me Kylie and all my other Deconstruction acts were gone, I knew it was time to go out on my own. Of course I asked Nick to come with me. He and I are a team, and I know our reputation in the industry is growing. We're Nick and Nicki. Nicki and Nick. He was reluctant to leave RCA at first. He's got a family to think about, so I understood why he might hesitate. But when I told Chairman John Preston I was leaving, he offered me Nick's job as Head of Promotions, to try to get me to stay.

'What about Nick? That's his job, isn't it?' I asked, only so I could watch the answer come out of his mouth.

'Don't worry about Nick, we've got plans for him,' he replied. I wasn't so sure.

Not only had they taken away a huge part of my roster, now they were offering me my best friend's job behind his back? It felt like MCA all over again. Only this time I didn't need to do a chart with coloured markers to prove my worth. Once I'd told Nick what John had said, there was no chance that he would stay, so we left together. He got in touch with his old plugger contact, Neil Ferris. That pair go way back. Neil has a strong reputation. He runs his own

PR company, the wonderfully named Brilliant! Everyone in the business says 'brilliant!' all the time; it's a perfect fit for a PR company. Neil had recently parted ways with Spanner, would you believe, the guy who was now handling the Deconstruction artists at RCA. Nick suggested to him that he might have a bit too much on his plate and Neil said he was right and would we like to join him? So we did. Timing is everything, as they say, and the time was exactly right.

It was a huge, terrifying leap for me to leave the security of a well-paid job in a big corporation like RCA and my little family there: Shacky, Richard, Narrinder, Tam and Carys. I've never seen myself as a risk-taker. I like to think I'm very much a true Capricorn – I'll keep going at things and I like to succeed, but I'm also quite pragmatic and sensible. I want things to be done properly. Stepping off that plank into the unknown waters of being my own boss was a moment of wildness for me that felt unfamiliar, but also totally right. Having Nick with me helped – he is such an ally, we work so well together – as did knowing I have the unerring support of Simon Fuller.

When I told Simon that Nick and I were leaving RCA, he said instantly that he'd bring all his acts, including the Spice Girls, to me at Brilliant! for their promotion. The girls had already said they wanted to work with me and he'd cut them a deal with Virgin that allowed them to take their publicity out of house. He had the same set-up with Annie Lennox, who we've all worked with so successfully – and who was there at that Japanese restaurant when we first talked about a girl group like the Spice Girls. So she came onto our roster as well. Nigel Martin-Smith told RCA that Take That's publicity would stay with me and Nick too. There was no way it wouldn't. When an act is that big there is very little a label can do to force their hand and we had a strong and fantastic relationship going. Gary Barlow even offered to finance us if we needed it (we didn't, but it was still extremely kind of him; that's the power of the Take That family, the TTs). So Nick and I joined Brilliant! PR with Annie Lennox, the new Robbie-less Take That and this up-and-coming girl group called the Spice Girls. I have fewer artists to look after, but my goodness the ones I've got are bloody good. It helps that the offices are super close in Acton as well. I can still walk to work at a push, although I am very fond of my new Mitsubishi Shogun. (My company car has increased in size, even if my roster hasn't.)

Driving home, finally, at 3 a.m. I've got the heating on full blast at my toes. I'm tired but I am wide awake. I wonder if Shacky is up. A new life has started for him, too. He's moved out to New York for a while. How many times have I driven this route over the years now? From north London to south, over the Westway, and home to my little flat. I know every traffic light, every lane I need to be in on this journey. It feels different tonight somehow. Like it's my own personal route and nothing is going to stop me.

18

Girls & Boys

The Spice Girls feel like an incredible gift that has been handed to me. I want to run with it, with them, and show the world what I can do. They're also turning out to be an education. They're teaching me girl power. I know it's a bit of a corny line, but I look at those girls and the way they handle situations and I'm in awe of what they have achieved so far. I've always thought I'm quite assertive and I think I've managed to hold my own in this industry, but they're another level; brazen, ballsy, and always true to themselves and who they are. They're all beautiful, but they're not selling themselves with their looks the way a lot of female performers may do. The charts are saturated with male-fronted bands at the moment. The whole Britpop thing is mostly boys: Oasis and Blur, Pulp and the Charlatans. It's great, the nineties is producing fantastic music, creating a moment in music history, not just in the UK but around the world. But for a girl band, and a pop one at that, to get in on the conversation and be taken seriously, they have to work twice as hard and be twice as talented as their male counterparts. I think the Spice Girls are going to be OK.

Breaking them has been an interesting journey for me as a publicist. My role is changing with this act, mainly because they have such a powerful message as well as their sound. That time when they came in to see me at RCA and blew me away, I decided the best way to promote them into radio and television would be to have them do the very same thing for producers and presenters. It's a new approach for me but I know they're the best people to promote themselves. When they're all together it truly feels like being in the presence of magic and they never let me down. They want this so much, I know I can rely on them to deliver (unlike some artists who let themselves down by being late or drunk, or who don't give a sh*t – or all three). When we first began to promote 'Wannabe', not everyone was buying it. Radio, especially some of the presenters at Radio 1 and 2, can be a little bit snobby about pop music, particularly when it's new pop music, by a girl band they've never heard of. Some people have even suggested it is manufactured, an off-the-shelf pop tune. But the girls wrote 'Wannabe' themselves, in partnership with Matt Rowe and Richard 'Biff' Stannard, known in the industry as Matt and Biff, and some of the best producers around.

Chris Evans has been particularly scathing about it, which isn't ideal. I took the girls in to the BBC to perform the 'Wannabe' routine for Suzi, the producer of *TFI Friday*, who is also Chris's girlfriend. *TFI Friday* is a Channel 4 show but as Chris is the breakfast presenter on Radio 1, everything he works on is based here. Even his producer for a show on a different channel has an office here. It's slightly awkward, but that's showbiz.

We had it all planned. The girls came barrelling into Suzi's office as they do, and started unleashing their mayhem. It was hilarious; they were writing on the whiteboards and being very 'Spice'. It was a pretty large office with an internal glass wall so people could see in. Just as the girls reached peak Spice, Chris walked past, banged hard on the window, and shouted: 'Fuck off back to *Live & Kicking* where you belong!'

It was quite a shocking moment and we stood there absolutely gobsmacked. The track was still going on the stereo and I rushed to switch it off. Did that just really happen? It took a second for us to work out whether it had been a joke or not, but there was no doubt that Chris was in a terrible mood and his words had been serious. Geri and Mel B wanted to run after him and find out what the problem was, but I put my foot down.

'No, leave it. Please leave this with me.' I don't often have to use my serious tone with them but I was pretty peeved at his display and there was no way anyone would be running after him after that. Suzi was very apologetic and tried to suggest he'd been joking, but he wasn't.

'Thank you for your time, Suzi. We'll leave it there.' I was mortified at this outburst. Why had I put us all through this when it was clear Chris wasn't going to take them seriously?

When I spoke to Nick about it later he told me Chris had also said on air that he thought the record was manufactured and likened them to Big Fun, a Stock Aitken and Waterman boy band no one has heard of in a while. Nick has asked the lawyers at Virgin to have a word with Radio 1. Hopefully, Chris will back off a bit. I certainly won't be plugging any of my acts to him again any time soon.

But even without Chris being difficult, radio is a tough one for a new pop act to break. The girls are such a visual experience, television is the way to get people interested. So I've been taking them around to all the television shows in person. They've got fantastic songs and that golden cross-generational appeal. They're great on camera, they can talk to people as well as perform. I knew *Surprise, Surprise!* would work well for them: Robson and Jerome and Kylie had been a huge success on the show for the same reason. So I gave Isobel Hutton a call, hoping to persuade her to put this un-known girl band on her show. It's one of the biggest watched shows on TV and historically doesn't put unknown artists on, only household names.

'OK Isobel, you've had Robson and Jerome, you've had Kylie on the show for me. I haven't been wrong yet, have I?

You've got to put this girl group on. Trust me on this one, they are amazing.'

Surprise, Surprise! gets around 12 million viewers every Sunday night, it's enormous. So Isobel couldn't put them on without seeing them. She told me to bring them in to meet her. Off we went in a little white van to LWT on the South Bank with the ghetto blaster. They all looked the part. I introduced them to Isobel, and was really effusive about how big they are going to be. They started to sing and before they could finish the first line Isobel was signalling for them to stop.

'Oh my God, not in here! Everyone's trying to work.'

Instead we went into the women's toilets and did it there. London Weekend Television does not have fancy toilets, let me tell you, but it turns out the acoustics aren't too shabby. There I was standing in the loos with five girls singing 'Wannabe' a cappella at Isobel Hutton. Thankfully they weren't fazed and Isobel loved it, so we cooked up a plan to get them on the show.

The way *Surprise, Surprise!* works is that people write in asking for Cilla Black to help them make a wish come true. We went through the postbag and found a letter from a teenage girl called Eleanor who had written in to Cilla saying she wanted to be a radio DJ. We arranged for her to spend the day broadcasting from Piccadilly Radio in Manchester and as part of her show, she interviewed the girls. They did their routine in the car park at the back of the radio station.

After the performance, Eleanor chatted to the girls and they told her about themselves. Melanie C said she likes football, Mel B said she's a northern nutter, Victoria said she likes shopping, Geri said she's a nutter as well, with method to her madness, and Emma said she likes cakes and doughnuts and pink. They also got across their different strengths and talked about how they were individuals but also loved being part of a group. I was so proud of them, and gave myself a small pat on the back for getting an unknown group on the biggest show on television. Time was, back at MCA, I wasn't allowed to talk to these shows because my bosses managed the prestigious television accounts. That has always been the joy for me of working with Nick Godwyn. Ever since he employed me at RCA he's been happy to let me loose on whatever it takes. It's good to prove him right with successes like these.

After *Surprise, Surprise!* we went to see the producers at *The Big Breakfast*. The girls are just so funny, they went in and sat on the boys' laps and spun the chairs round, threw things off the desk. It was carnage. It works though because everyone in the office stops what they are doing and watches, they can't believe what's happening. And the girls can cut it. You can't see any strings attached to them. They are off on their own, a force to be reckoned with, and underneath it all is the pride they have for their message and their music.

It's a very different experience to working with Take That. The wardrobe, hair and make-up requirements are massive, for starters. Plus the bills that come with it all! Whether we're shooting a video or off in a Transit van to sing to someone in the toilets, the girls all need a lot longer in the chair before making any kind of appearance. I need to book more make-up artists and stylists. I can't have just one doing them all because it takes so long. And the girls each have their own identity, whereas the boys always have more of a common theme. And of course the girls have more interest in what they will wear (although most of it comes from the high street, to give them credit) and look like. The boys are happy to be semi-glammed and directed on outfits, often with Mark steering the look, whereas the girls have their own very clear vision. But the major difference is the way they are when they have free time. Obviously the girls aren't quite on the same level as Take That (though who knows, one day) but even so, when they finish filming or doing a performance they usually want to get home and have an early night or see their boyfriends. They're quite sweet really, not rock'n'roll at all. They're dedicated to the band and very focused, but their friends and family play a huge role too. You don't have to worry about any of them disappearing or ending up somewhere they shouldn't be. The boys are different . . .

There's a sweet spot where these two groups cross over, and it is in their passion and performance, the quality of their work. They're all making great, fresh pop. Pop has a bad reputation for being somehow less than other types of music. Too silly and frivolous. But 'pop' is short for 'popular' and that's exactly what they are all about. Popular music. Entertaining everyone. Today, tomorrow, and hopefully for decades. Having such widespread appeal, to me, is a far greater achievement for an artist than only appealing to a small group. Each to their own, I guess. But no music snobbery here. I'm a proud pop tart.

The Spice Girls and Take That met recently at the Brit Awards, actually. Officially I was there looking after Take That, who performed 'How Deep Is Your Love', a cover of the classic and beautiful Bee Gees number. It was a gorgeous, gentle performance, with very pared-back staging, minimal but impactful. The song is all about those lyrics. The boys were wearing big white shirts, untucked, and black trousers; they didn't even have stools to sit on this time. No one can accuse us of blowing the budget with that one. Afterwards we sat at our big round table, buckets of champagne on ice, beers, vodka, wine. I don't generally drink at these things if I'm on duty, but with free champagne flowing it's hard not to. I'm not a big drinker but I'm never going to say no to champagne. I'll always have one or two at the end of the night, when I know the hard work is done. It's very vibey on the floor at the Brits and often it's the first time some acts have met their own idols (or if you're Blur and Oasis, their nemeses!) in the flesh. There are lots of famous people rushing around, hugging, laughing, gossiping and getting lairy. It's incredibly loud.

Anyway the girls were there at the awards as well. They weren't performing as they're not enough of a big deal to do that yet, but they'd been invited by the record label. It's a good opportunity to schmooze and meet people. Obviously they were all excited and when they saw me they came bounding over in all their finery to say hello. Although of course I knew it wasn't me they wanted to talk to. Oh no. And the boys were very pleased to meet them, shall we say. There were a few tongues hanging out around that table. There I was playing gooseberry between one of the biggest boy bands ever and a girl group I'm hoping might achieve a modicum of similar success. Who knows?

19

Together Forever

The Warner Bros. office is in South Kensington and it's a short walk back down the high street to where my car is parked. I hope the car will be OK. I've traded the Shogun for a BMW soft top in British racing green with a touch of sparkle in the finish, if you please. It is my pride and joy and I drive it everywhere. Although there is talk of introducing a congestion charge for London, I can't see how that is going to work.

Nick and I pass by Kensington Market as we walk to the car. The place is looking a bit the worse for wear these days. Such a shame, it was a real Mecca for young people and youth culture in its time. It didn't matter what your tribe was – goths, New Romantics, punks, rude girls, ravers – everyone could find something to wear, get a tattoo, have their nose or somewhere else pierced, or just hang out gawping at everyone. And it wasn't only vintage clothes. There were some great new designers as well: Jean Paul Gaultier, John Galliano, Paul Smith, Red or Dead. The music was always blasting out of course. I wonder if it will stay the distance. The high street is changing. Quite a few of the old brands are disappearing – no more Ravel, no more Kookai or Dolcis. There are rumours Our Price is on the way out. You can buy CDs on the internet now and they are much cheaper because the sellers don't have big overheads like they do with shops. I can't get my head around the idea that record shops won't exist, but some people think it could happen.

We are in buoyant mood though. We've just had a great meeting at Warner Bros. They want us to do the promo for Eric Clapton's new album, *River of Tears*. Eric Clapton! He doesn't want to use the in-house PR team apparently, so they've called us in. Nick and Nicki to the rescue. We get these referrals from record labels occasionally. All record labels have their own in-house promo teams, like we were at RCA, but sometimes it doesn't work out or they are too busy on another project at that time, and so they call in an independent. We're an established, safe pair of hands and we don't get mixed up in company politics. It's been interesting to work from the outside and look in to the record labels after years of being part of them; to see things from a different angle, what works and what doesn't. The corporate set-up can seem quite old-fashioned now, all the meetings and protocols! As Head of Television and Head of Promotions, Nick and I were regularly required to attend endless meetings at RCA that we didn't need to be at. Now we've gone 'indie', as they say, we can focus purely on the job. It's all about the promotion in our book.

That said, it's not always an entirely liberated experience. During this morning's meeting, Nick had to stop the client and point out that I was the person in the room that he should be talking to, not Nick. The guy had obviously assumed I was Nick's secretary and was directing his questions about Eric Clapton's promo to Nick. That's the great thing about Nick: it would never occur to him to let that slide. He stopped the guy mid-sentence and pointed at me:

'Can I just say, I don't know why you are talking to me here. This one is the expert.'

I laughed. I don't care who they talk to as long as they pay the invoice. But I can think of plenty of men who would be happy to let a client think I'm their assistant. Luckily I don't work with any of them these days.

Another bonus of Nick and I joining Neil Ferris at Brilliant! has been picking up some of his existing clients. He has a great roster of synth-pop acts like Erasure and Depeche Mode and is in talks with Moby's management. It means that with our acts and Neil's we have a lot of very highly respected, successful talent on the list. The most discerning managers in the industry are clamouring to get us to work with their acts. So much so that we don't need to do any self-promotion at all. There was a call from a reporter at *Music Week* a couple of weeks ago, wanting to do a story on us. But we haven't even called them back. We genuinely don't need the publicity, which of course makes us even more interesting and desirable to the managers. Besides, I'm not interested in being in front of the camera.

I drop Nick back at the office, waving at him from the soft top as I leave.

'Hope your perm doesn't fall out!' he shouts at me from across the street. Cheeky sod. All this driving with the roof down is wonderful but it's wreaking havoc with my supposedly beach wave perm. We are like brother and sister these days. We can finish each other's sentences, each of us knows what the other one is thinking. Sometimes I wonder if people think something is going on between us, but there isn't and there never has been. It's just one of those magical connections between two people, and the best bit is we get to work together every single day. We fill the spaces for each other. If I need to handle a particularly difficult artist or manager, I know I can call Nick for back-up, while he knows I'll cover the acts he's less close to, do all the detail with the live performances and filming.

Shacky loves Nick too. Now he's back from New York and we're together, it's handy for him having us both just over the bridge, as he's stepped into Nick's old role at RCA. He took it when he came back to London so we could be together. Classic Chappers! Please don't call me contrary, but I finally decided he was the one for me when he'd moved to the other side of the world. Luckily for me, he came back. Gave up a massive job opportunity over there and everything.

I get home and he's made dinner (a delicious salad and a piece of pan-fried salmon). I'm definitely not a cook, I'm the first to admit that, but Shacky is and he is always making something for me. I think he needs to know I'm well nourished. I always get him his fresh coffee in the morning in return. He loves his morning coffee. It's the small things, isn't it? There is a kindness between us that I've realised I haven't experienced before in a relationship, it's a different league. It still surprises me every day that we are together. We're so different in so many ways, but increasingly it also feels like we have always been together.

We devour our food and get ready to head out. We're off to see *The Mousetrap* tonight. Another bonus of being an indie, Brilliant! handles the promo for several West End theatres, TV shows and events. The Brits, the Mercurys, ITV's *Talking Telephone Numbers* with Phillip Schofield, Emma Forbes and Claudia Winkleman. We're doing *The Big Breakfast*, even some live events staged by Midland Bank at the disused Battersea Power Station. They're all on our roster and I am making the most of the tickets I get as a result. It requires the same plugging skill set: building relationships with the media and getting the shows on television and radio. But it's a whole new area for me and one I'm very happy to be exploring. Theatre runs in my blood, after all, and I'm still just as excited by live performances as I have ever been.

Later on, in the taxi home, mind blown by the longest-running show in theatreland, I get a text message from Nick.

'Do we know a Robert Stigwood? Malcolm says he's called three times today. Says it's an Isle of Wight number? Ps. How's your perm x'

Neither of us knows Robert Stigwood.

'No, sorry lovely. Never heard of him. Perm says hi! x'

At home Shacky and I are both bashing our heads in my tiny bathroom in the eaves as we clean our teeth.

'I want to buy my own house.' There, I've said it out loud. It's been on my mind for a while. 'I want somewhere bigger and I can get the mortgage now with what I'm earning at Brilliant! And if I buy somewhere you could live there?'

'No way,' he says, still brushing vigorously. Well. That wasn't the answer I was expecting. I thought he'd be up for that, I have to say. I have stopped mid-brush to look at him.

He spits his toothpaste out, rinses, and stands up so we are looking at each other side by side in the little mirror above the sink. 'But I will buy somewhere with you. We'll go halves. In it together.'

20

Riders On The Storm

It is chaos in the office today. We're having to get new computers put in so we can write the symbol for the artist formerly known as Prince with our keyboards. He changed his name to this 'love' symbol – apparently it's a combination of the gender signs for male and female – and now everyone has to refer to him as that. But we haven't worked with him before, so no one has it on their computer and we can't write his name, there's not even a word for it that anyone can say.

His old label, Warner Bros., has sent us floppy disks with the symbol on, but the company needs new computers to use them. No one knows why he changed his name, although there is speculation that he fell out with the label and changing his name to a symbol was an attempt to get out of his contract, or at least make life very difficult for them. The statement that arrived with the floppy disk says: 'It's all about thinking in new ways, tuning in 2 a new free-quency.' It's a bit of a pain but on the bright side, we are now working with ♀. (Let's just call him Prince for ease.)

Prince has a new album coming out with his new label, EMI. It's aptly titled *Emancipation*, and we've been asked to do the promotion for it in the UK. We've organised a huge launch for it at the Orangery, a beautiful eighteenth-century location in Kensington Gardens. Prince isn't going to be there – he hardly does any promotion and has already declined to do any television, which is a shame but not a surprise. So we needed to organise the launch somewhere fabulous enough and with enough good coffee, smoked salmon and bagels that it would entice journalists and photographers to come along at 6 a.m. to see him beamed in via a screen. Princess Diana lunches at the Orangery a lot, it has cachet. It also has a car park in front of it so photographers and the press, anyone with equipment, can get there easily. So much of this job is about making it easier for people – while also setting up a first-class venue for a huge new album reveal from an icon.

Thankfully, the launch went extremely well. There were no technical hitches, lots of great feedback from the press and enthusiasm for his new work. Prince played a couple of tracks and talked about splitting with the record label and finally having some freedom to make the music that he wants to make. The man is so prolific. It felt like this new material was an important moment in Prince's evolution. For me personally, nothing will ever beat the *Around the World in a Day* album. I remember listening to 'Raspberry Beret' driving into college with my bestie Krista. But I'm delighted he's making new music.

I'm not sure why he's changed his mind, though I like to think it had something to do with the reaction to the global launch we organised and how excited the world is about the new album. Whatever it is, after the launch I get a message to say Prince has decided that he'll come over to London and do *Top of the Pops* after all.

Suddenly I was going to be looking after one of pop music's greatest artists. It reminded me that this is why I work in the music industry, I get to be up close to genius like this.

So now I'm in the office trying to work out how to write his name. I get a fax from Prince's American management team detailing his rider. Some stars are famous for their over-the-top riders: Mariah Carey demands Cristal champagne and bendy (not straight) straws to sip it with, air purifiers and couches in dark colours (no busy patterns). My favourite is from Iggy Pop and the Stooges, who write hilarious, long riders stipulating preposterous things like a Bob Hope impersonator and seven dwarves in pointy hats.

Fortunately for me, or so I think, Prince's rider seems to be mostly about food. He wants a very specific coffee machine, an old-fashioned fruit juicer, lavender and jasmine tea, vitamin B12 shots (what are they??) and all sorts of things

I've never heard of. He also stipulates that everything should be wrapped in cling film. But I figure this is all part of the rich tapestry and so a few days later I go out and get it all. Everything he wants, right down to the shots. Bearing in mind that *Top of the Pops* is filmed in Borehamwood and the area is not known for its cultural diversity, I get a personal chef to prepare all the food he's demanded (everything vegetarian, no meat allowed near him), and put it all out on a trestle table, like the kind you use for wallpapering. It is all there for him. I have spent a fortune on it, hundreds and hundreds of pounds. I have lugged it all into the studio and laid it out on the table like some kind of Last Supper buffet for the Purple One.

On the day of filming, Prince walks in to the dressing room, looking divine as always. He gives me the slightest of nods, takes one look at the table heaving under the weight of his rider, then turns away from it and doesn't touch a thing for the rest of the evening. Not a nibble, not a nut.

'Would you like anything to eat?' I don't say his name because I don't want to get it wrong.

'No thank you.' He smiles and makes direct eye contact with me. Some people have told me he might not look me in the eye but he does and even smiles. His voice is so delicate. He is one of the most dynamic, groundbreaking and prolific performers of all time. And yet he looks so small and fragile.

He is travelling with his fiancée Mayte Garcia, this beautiful woman who was his backing singer and is now engaged

to him. You can tell they are so in love; they're very affection-
ate with one another, holding hands and kissing. She doesn't
want any of the world's hardest-to-achieve rider either.

He says: 'Mayte's mom will be here in a moment, she
might want something.'

I don't know why I say it – I think I'm using humour to
mask my nerves or something – but it just comes out: 'Ooh,
you've got to pay close attention to the mother, because
that's what you're marrying. That's what she'll look like
when you're both old.' I laugh, even though very quickly I
realise that no one else is.

And then Mayte's mum walks in. I glance across to him,
and I don't think I'll ever forget his face.

Still, he seems happy. Goes out and does quite a gentle
performance of 'The Holy River', wearing his sunglasses
all the way through. He strikes me as a gentle person all
round, not the man that you think of as strutting around
and being quite sexual. I suppose I should have guessed that
he wasn't going to eat anything much from that rider. It's
probably a generic one that goes out wherever he goes. It's
easier for them to ask for everything than nothing. It will
all come home with me tonight anyway. My fridge will be
packed full. At least I won't need to go shopping for a few
days. Small win.

21

Let's Dance

'Everyone say hello to Nicki's Aunty Liz. She's over from Australia!'

The whole crowd cheers and the big lights are flashing all over the arena. I can only imagine what Aunty Liz is feeling right now. David Bowie has just given her a shout-out, live at Wembley. She certainly won't have been expecting that.

I've brought her here with me as I know she loves David Bowie and I want to treat her while she's visiting. I introduce her to him before he goes on stage. 'Hello Aunty Liz,' he says, beaming at her.

He was smoking a cigarette just before he went on and he handed it to me as he walked on stage. I'm wishing I'd kept it now. I didn't know what to do with it so I just stubbed it out in one of the ashtrays backstage. Chappers, you fool! That had been in David Bowie's mouth! Why didn't I keep it? It just doesn't occur to me in the moment and to be honest I am still a bit nervous – OK, utterly star-struck – by him. He has an aura about him, but in person he's kind and elegant. And now he's said hello to my Aunty Liz again, on stage, to everyone at Wembley Arena! Liz won't know what to do with herself when I meet her after the show.

I'm getting an incredible view of it all from the side of the stage. It's still what I consider to be one of the greatest privileges of my job, being able to watch artists at work from this viewpoint. Seeing the audience living in the moment and perhaps having one of the best nights of their lives. Sometimes when we were touring with Take That, I would sit in the area right by the stage. Just me and a security guard. Occasionally one of the boys would glance down and give me a wink or a wave, that was special. God, I sound like a fan. Shame I didn't get my Kodak Brownie out. It just wouldn't be the done thing.

This is the second time I've met David Bowie this week. He's over in London promoting his album, *Outside*. His UK manager Alan Edwards asked Nick and me to look after his promo for him. We've known Alan for years – he's a legend in the PR world and has branched out into management. He needs a team he can trust, it's David Bowie for goodness' sake. So we got David on *Top of the Pops*. It wasn't the hardest booking, I have to admit.

I greeted them at the studio a few hours before filming

for *Top of the Pops*, as I would with any act. Iman walked in like a goddess, making me feel about three feet tall. She was dressed head to toe in skintight denim, a total vision, very friendly but ever so quiet and polite. Then David introduced his manager/personal assistant, Coco Schwab. Everyone in the business knows about Coco, and how fiercely she protects David. She's been with him for over forty years and there are stories – or should it be legends – about how she helped him kick drugs and saved his life in the 1970s. I was more than a little apprehensive about dealing with her, and let's just say she lived up to her reputation. I got the full-on Rottweiler treatment from her. She's very demanding. She didn't want anyone around him. She wanted to know who was going to be where and when. Did we have his rider (Lavazza coffee and Marlboro Reds)? What time was the rehearsal? Where could she make calls? She really kept me on my toes, had me running around the studios and dressing rooms. I spent the whole time with my huge box file from the office in my arms. I'd brought literally every piece of paperwork, every form, every licence, every certificate we own with me, so that I could produce it if Coco asked for it.

David was a true gentleman throughout. I tried every single shop in Borehamwood for his Lavazza coffee and had to tell him that his favourite brand could not be located.

'I'm so sorry David, they obviously don't drink a lot of Lavazza in Borehamwood. I've looked everywhere for you

and there's none to be found. I've got you some of the supermarket's own brand instead.'

I could feel Coco's glare through the back of my head. But
David was so calm and serene.

'Don't worry about it, Nicki. This will be fine.' He smiled,
his eyes hypnotising me as he spoke. This man is an absolute legend and here I am blathering on about supermarket
coffee.

Phew.

It was a classy performance of 'Strangers When We Meet'.
He looked iconic in his big overcoat and sunglasses. Then afterwards, I saw Coco and David in the corridor and signalled
to them as I needed just to tie up a couple of things before
they left. Iman was in the car and they were all getting ready
to go. This was the umpteenth time David Bowie had done
Top of the Pops, he's an old hand, so I knew there wouldn't
be any hanging around. No glugging of the free beers and
sausage rolls for Mr Bowie. Coco strode up to me, as I was
still clutching my giant file for dear life, and said:

'Now, you!'

I could feel my face reddening as I prepared to take the
force of her reprimands, which somehow always sound
worse in an American accent.

'You! Have been amazing this evening. We've had a great
day, thank you so much for looking after us.'

I felt so relieved I nearly slid down the wall onto the floor.

And off they walked into the grey car park, past a few of

the *EastEnders* cast who were standing having a cigarette by the bins, some of them looking at him twice as he walked past. For a brief moment I wanted to run after him and say *David, wait! Why don't you all stay and we can have a few drinks and a chat?* What I would have given to spend some time with him, perhaps even ask him for a photo. I remembered that he has probably met a hundred people like me, more, on his many times around the earth. I am just one plugger, publicist, whatever you want to call me, on the conveyor belt of the music industry.

It's funny. The older and more successful I get, the more that thought occurs to me. That I'm just another cog in the wheel. Maybe it's because I'm dealing with older and more successful artists, people who have achieved so much, that I feel more in awe of them. Now I'm working with more established acts, not only youngsters who I'm with from the start, there's definitely a different relationship. Maybe it's because the industry is changing so much. The internet is opening so many new doors for everyone in this business. It makes me wonder what the future holds. Earlier on I was earwigging while David was talking to some of the tech guys in the studio about the World Wide Web and how he thinks a revolution is coming. He seemed really excited by it all, reckoned artists would be able to create and put out their own music one day, all on the internet.

I'm certainly getting to work with some big names these days. That man who called the office, Robert Stigwood?

Turns out he was the manager of the Bee Gees and Cream. He put on *Hair, Jesus Christ Superstar* and *Grease*, all the big musicals of the 1970s and 80s. One of the greatest musical impresarios of the age had been calling my office in Acton to speak to me and Nick! I should have known and recognised that name from the start. He wants us to help him with a new stage show of *Saturday Night Fever*. He arrived at the office in his Rolls-Royce the other day, and we all went for breakfast to discuss it.

No matter how everyday this stuff becomes for me, it's still never entirely normal. And it's never anywhere near normal for my mum and dad, Shelley and my best friend from school days Krista, who all still love to hear about my escapades.

I had Krista in stitches the other day, telling her about attending the Prince's Trust Awards in Manchester recently.

It was the twenty-first anniversary gala awards, in front of the Prince of Wales, to celebrate everything the charity does. We had a whole raft of our artists in that show: Cathy Dennis, Gary Barlow doing a song from his new solo album, *Open Road*, and the Spice Girls doing 'Say You'll Be There'. And we had Phil Collins. Now, Nick has a relationship with Phil from his days at Virgin, before RCA, and we are doing the promo for his new album, *Dance Into the Light*. So we had a full house, all our best artists were performing there that night. It illustrates how well we are doing at the moment, and the whole Brilliant! team was out in force to cover the night.

At any of these events, I often get asked by one act if they can meet another. Just because someone is famous doesn't mean they can't also be fans. And on this night Gary Barlow, as you can imagine, was extremely keen to meet Phil Collins. Even I was a little bit overcome when I heard Phil Collins was coming. Genesis was the first concert I ever went to, at the NEC all those years ago. So I knew that Gary, as a songwriter, would be desperate to meet Phil. I asked Phil if I could introduce Gary, and he, lovely man that he is, said: 'Yeah, yeah, bring him in.'

I took Gary into Phil's dressing room and they got on like a house on fire. As you'd expect they had lots to talk about and they chatted away for twenty minutes. Eventually I had to say: 'Look, guys, you both have to rehearse now, I'm going to have to drag you out!'

Gary shook Phil's hand and stood up to leave and as he was opening the door, Phil said: 'By the way, where are the rest of the boys?'

Gary said: 'Sorry?'

Phil: 'Where's the rest of the band?'

Gary and I looked at each other for a second thinking he's taking the mickey but then realised that Phil hasn't got a clue that they split up eighteen months earlier. To be fair he's been living in Switzerland, in his own little bubble.

Poor Gary, looking slightly disappointed that Phil Collins wasn't abreast of his news, said: 'Ah, we split up a year and a half ago Phil!' and left, giving me a quick roll of his eyes.

Phil pulled a face at me that said *Oops!*

I reassured him that it was fine and that actually, I had another favour to ask him before he went into rehearsal.

'The Spice Girls really want to meet you!'

His face lit up and he said without hesitation:

'Spice Girls? Yeah? Bring 'em in!'

The next thing, the girls came charging in and did what they always do: jumped on top of him, started kissing his head, squashing his face up, Emma was in his minibar opening bottles of gin, Mel C had one leg in the air, Mel B was sat on his lap doing her hair in his mirror. Obviously Phil was in his element, loving it. These five gorgeous young women just couldn't get enough of him. They were going: 'Oh Phil we love you, we love you!'

Then Victoria asked him very politely: 'Phil, can I possibly have your autograph?'

Of course he immediately agreed. 'Where do I sign?' All jaunty and pleased with himself because this beautiful woman wants his autograph.

Victoria said: 'Oh brilliant thanks. It's for my mum, she loves you.'

Poor Phil, his face was a picture.

I said: 'Right you lot, leave him alone, you've got to get ready now!' and got them out of the dressing room. Just before I followed them he whispered: 'Thanks Nicki. They're great, aren't they? Who are they again?'

Then of course there was the incident where they kissed

Prince Charles after the show in the foyer. It's been all over the papers, Prince Charles looking bashful and pretending not to enjoy it. They're so naughty. We had practised the whole line-up earlier that day and gone through all the etiquette with the people from the Palace about what they were supposed to do. And of course they ignored all of that and totally Spiced him. Mel B asked him if they could come to the Palace for dinner. Geri, who was in a very revealing cheerleader-type outfit, told him he's sexy and patted his bum. The heir to the throne! She meant it as well. There was no filter. They couldn't have been further from the agreed protocol if they'd tried. It was risky and it's a wonder they weren't all wrestled to the ground by security, but it was also brilliant, and of course it made all the headlines.

Krista asked me if I got a telling-off from anyone at the Palace. I did get pulled up by one of his press team who complained that it wasn't really how it was meant to go. All I could say was:

'I think we all knew exactly how it was going to go. It's the Spice Girls.'

22

Down In Africa

I'm in Pretoria, South Africa, with the Spice Girls and they've just been chatting with and hugging Nelson Mandela outside his presidential residence. I don't really know how else to say it. That's what's just happened. The girls have done their whole Spice thing on him, they've all been kissing him and holding his hands, and he loved it. He actually said: 'This is one of the greatest moments in my life', and told the crowd that the Spice Girls are his heroes. Then he said he was an old man and Geri chimed in with: 'You're only as old as the woman you feel, and I'm twenty-five, Nelson.' I've had a few surreal moments in my career but I think that tops the list.

We're here for a charity concert, supporting the Nation's Trust, a collaboration between the UK and South Africa that helps South African entrepreneurs. All that flirting with

Prince Charles at the Prince's Trust Awards earlier in the year and the global headlines it generated obviously caught the attention of the organisers and the girls were asked to perform. Prince Charles is here as well, with young Prince Harry, the poor boy is looking most uncomfortable in a suit and tie. It's one of the first times we've all seen him since Diana died earlier in the year. It still breaks my heart to think about it. I get why Prince Charles has brought Harry along – if anyone can put a smile on that young man's face it's the Spice Girls.

Simon can't be here as he has seriously injured his back and is on bed rest, so I'm here to make sure everything runs smoothly. The world's press has also turned out in force and the girls are on winning form. After this photo shoot they'll go to Johannesburg to perform in front of 60,000 people, then we'll all be bussed back to Sun City, South Africa's answer to Las Vegas, where we are all staying, and do press interviews for several hours. As always, I am impressed by their stamina and willingness to push on through. Gruelling isn't the right word because it's such a magical experience, and who would ever complain about being part of such an important cultural moment? But it's non-stop, and in searing temperatures.

After the show, a large group of journalists is waiting on the veranda at the hotel. It's my job to oversee the questions and ensure the reporters get what they need from the girls. Talking as a group is something they've spent a lot of time perfecting. We did some media training sessions at the very beginning with Andi Peters, the BBC presenter, to help them get it right. It's quite an art when you're in a five-piece like this, not to talk over and interrupt each other. But they do it well. Each one of them says something fresh and allows the others to talk, and they can navigate even the most obnoxious questions. They're one act I don't have to worry about on that front. They seem to just fit, they talk and perform as one.

Everyone has finally had their turn and they're wrapping up. I can tell the girls are tired and distracted now. They need some downtime. They've also got a private meeting arranged, apparently. They're all still in their costumes – those huge platform trainers must be melting onto their feet. As they're on their way out, a reporter says: 'I just need to ask a couple more questions.' There is always one. The girls are all flagging, I can see it, and I don't blame them for continuing to walk away. But Geri turns around and I look at her and say, with a face that knows I'm pushing my luck: 'Can you do just one more little bit for me?' And without hesitating she looks me in the eye and says: 'Of course I will.'

They all have an impressive work ethic. I don't think I've ever met harder grafters. And it isn't just about the pursuit of fame, it's about being authentically successful, and true to their creativity. Geri and Mel B certainly drive a lot of the conversations with Simon in management meetings. It's always one of them asking: 'What's the game plan? What can we do?' They are all invested in their success, more so than many of the acts I've worked with, and they want to be all over the decision-making process. But like any band, they need Simon and a management team around them, because they need someone who can see the bigger picture in this situation. Sometimes when you're in the middle of it, you can't see the wood for the trees. I do admire how they are all so committed to each other, to the group. All that talk about friendship never ends, they really mean it. They have each other's back.

Sun City is like a theme park, all casinos and swimming pools. It's not the real South Africa. But a small bonus is that it backs onto the Pilanesberg National Park, one of the country's largest national parks, situated inside an old volcano crater and promising encounters with all kinds of wildlife including the 'big five' (not the Spice Girls, the other, safari big five). It continues to be extremely important to me that I don't simply give my artists downtime while they are travelling, but meaningful and memorable experiences. They are young people who have not yet had the chance to see the world and experience different cultures. Nor have I! So I've suggested we get up at 5 a.m. tomorrow to go on a safari in the Pilanesberg National Park. No one has any safari clothes with them – we're all just in shorts and T-shirts – so the next morning we don't exactly look the part as we clamber onto an open-top four-by-four with the park warden and set off.

I am acutely aware in this moment, thundering across

the African landscape in an open-top truck with the Spice Girls as the sun rises, that this will always be a highlight for me, not only of my career but my life. It's a true 'pinch me' moment. Forget the Spice Girls, I'm actually on a safari.

After driving for a short while we slow down. In the distance an elephant is coming towards us. We are all saying things like 'Oh my goodness' and 'Look at that', absolutely in awe of this incredible beast. You think you know what they look like but in real life it's a different matter. The colours and the motion, the sound, everything, is quite ethereal and you feel very small in the presence of it all. Concerts and press trips and merchandising suddenly seem extremely insignificant. We are stunned into silence at this vision. And the warden says: 'Everyone be quiet, everyone be still.'

Then out from behind the elephant appears its calf. It's a mother and her baby. She isn't walking, she is charging towards us.

'Oh my God. Oh my God.' We all switch from awe to panic. A huge wild animal is coming for us.

The driver and the warden exchange rapid words in Zulu and the driver reverses at high speed. When there's enough distance between us and the mother elephant, he swings the truck around and we exit the park in a cloud of dust. It's not yet 7 a.m. and we all return to our beds for an hour, all with more adrenaline on board than when we left.

Japan, Hong Kong, the States. We've been all over the world now doing promotions and performing. In Los

Angeles, we stayed at the Four Seasons Hotel. I think that is the swankiest hotel I've stayed at, with my acts or without them. Gorgeous, mid-century Beverly Hills glamour. I don't know how they got the budget for that but I was more than happy to go with it. They filmed the video for 'Say You'll Be There' with Vaughan Arnell, who worked on 'Back for Good', in the Mojave Desert just outside LA. They used my red gingham check bikini to tie a poor man up in one scene (their idea!). My bikini's claim to fame.

Another time we all went up in a hot-air balloon for a Saturday-morning programme on ITV called *Massive*. Denise van Outen was going to interview them and we were all set for it, but on the morning we were due to go up it was deemed too foggy, so we went off for breakfast at a nearby Little Chef. After a few hours of kicking our heels we managed to get off the ground and do the interview, all of us crammed into a giant wicker basket hundreds of feet in the air. But apparently it's unusual to go up at that time of day and the captain started to struggle to get us down; something to do with thermals, and not the silk variety. In the end some people working in a field below had to help us down with the tethers. Goodness knows what they must have thought. They were there doing their work one minute and the next they were pulling the Spice Girls down from the sky.

On a trip to Japan they got off their flight at 6 a.m. having had no sleep, went straight to a hotel, ignored the brutal jet lag, had showers, got into their outfits and performed on *Top of the Pops* via a live link-up to the UK from the Naritasan Shinsho-ji temple, in 36-degree heat. We did it there because it was the closest temple to the airport and we needed to get it done in time for the live link-up. I'd taken some big cardboard *Top of the Pops* logo boards on the plane and I had to tie them on to anything I could find so viewers could see the logo. They say it's not all glamour at the top. It really isn't!

They are a truly global act now and it is my privilege to be here for the ride, although as with Take That, I always know I can get off when I'm feeling sick. The girls are on it 24/7, acutely aware that they need to be professional and on show all the time. As I learned with Robbie in his Glastonbury episode, there is very little scope for having an off day when you're a pop star. And increasingly there is very little privacy for any of them.

Victoria has been seeing David (Beckham, the footballer) for a while now and we've been trying to help them keep it under wraps. Not because there is anything wrong with them seeing each other but because they want some privacy. If he's playing football and we are away or filming, she asks me to find out what the scores are from Shacky, especially if it's a Saturday as we're often rehearsing for a major TV show in the afternoon that will air in the evening. Obviously she can't call David, and she doesn't really want to call other people and let it be known they're together because it is still quite undercover, so I ring Shacky for her – he doesn't even support Manchester United – and ask: 'How's he doing? How's he playing? What's the score?' Then I feed it back to her. Last weekend Shacky arranged for Victoria and Mel C to join him in the RCA box at Chelsea so Victoria could watch David play. I don't know who was more excited, Victoria seeing David or Shacky meeting all the players.

These are five individual young women with personal lives and opinions and partners and families. Managing them, especially from a distance, is not without its challenges for Simon. I've been aware of, shall we say, difficulties for some time now. They are this huge explosion, all around the world, and keeping any kind of control over it is becoming increasingly difficult.

This week it came to quite a head. Like Simon, I can't be there every minute of every day with the girls. I am the co-owner of Brilliant! and I have other artists on my roster whom I respect and whose promotions we take care of. Take That of course, but also Cathy Dennis. She had her own successful career a few years ago, releasing a couple of great tracks, 'Touch Me' and 'Too Many Walls'. She was one of the UK's most successful and biggest-selling artists in the US for a while. But the limelight wasn't for her and she's now focusing on writing. She is a phenomenal songwriter. She and Simon Fuller are working on a kind of virtual artist at the moment, Alta B. It's quite futuristic, like a music robot. Always ahead of the curve is Mr Fuller.

So I needed to spend some time catching up with my other

artists. While we both work television, MTV has always been Nick's baby. He goes way back with MTV, before the RCA days. They have an annual awards ceremony, kind of like the Brits, and this year it was in Rotterdam. I am still getting over my last MTV Awards in Berlin, with Robbie and Prince's 'doctor', so we decided that Nick would cover the MTV awards with the girls, and give me some time in London at the office to catch up. The girls were nominated in the Viewer's Choice and Dance Video categories, and performed 'Spice Up Your Life' during the event. It was a visual feast of a production: the girls have the most brilliant percussionist, fire and incredible lighting on the stage. They really stole the show, quite an achievement at that event. And as you can imagine, everyone who is anyone was there, all the big international acts. Nick said all eyes were on the girls. Even Foo Fighters went to watch them practise earlier in the day. He'd had to fight off a cameraman who'd been trying to take pictures up their skirts. How disgusting is that? Nick said he shoved him against the wall and made him drop his camera by stamping on the guy's feet, a technique he'd learned from the security team we used for Take That. Nick would protect any of our acts like that, I know. Their safety and wellbeing is a matter of personal pride for us both. We are trusted by these people to look after them. It's never just a job.

Of course the aftershow partying was set to be off the scale. No one parties harder than a bunch of stars post-awards ceremony. But Simon had given strict instructions to Nick that the girls needed to stay in a different hotel to the other guests and go straight back there afterwards, away from where all the parties were happening. As the dodgy snapper had proved earlier on, the hysteria around the girls can very quickly get out of hand and he wanted them to get some rest and peace and quiet. We knew this wouldn't go down well with them, but it wasn't something I could influence; I was in London and they were in Rotterdam.

Then this morning at 8 a.m. I got a call. I'd gone into the office early with the plan to get ahead for the week. It was blissfully quiet, and I was at my desk on the mezzanine floor we've had put in recently to create more space. There's such a lot of equipment and vinyl, CDs and cassettes to store. So I have a desk up in the sky now and I can look down over the boardroom. When the phone rang at that time I knew something was up. No one rings me on my direct line at that time on a Monday.

It was Geri.

'Hi Geri! Are you OK? How was last night? It looked incredible.' Trying not to let her know how gutted I was I hadn't gone.

She skipped the niceties: 'Are you on your own, Nicki?'

'Yes. Why? What's happened?'

'We've sacked Simon.'

I paused. The words were a shock but also felt in some ways like something I'd known was going to happen for a while. They'd mentioned a couple of issues when we were in Africa, and now I was thinking about it they'd also had a couple of private meetings over there that I hadn't been part of. But events and the sheer chaos of their schedule had eclipsed any sense of discontent at the time and I had put it to the back of my mind. That was a mistake.

'Geri, you're on a flight in a couple of hours and we're going to be rehearsing *An Audience with the Spice Girls* to-night. Oh, and Simon's brother Kim is going to be there as he's writing it, remember? Shall we talk about this when you get back?' I was trying to buy some time so I could talk to Nick, and to Simon.

'No, we want you to know we've been up all night, the lawyer's sent a legal letter to his lawyer. We've got rid of Simon Fuller.'

23

This I Swear

'Should I send a private plane for you?' Simon asks.

'No!' I screech, a little too loudly. I am in Sainsbury's buying toilet roll on my way home from the office, and Simon Fuller wants to know if I need a private jet to get to Italy. It's a high/low kind of life.

Nick and I are flying out to see Simon tomorrow. He is devastated about the girls. He has had major back surgery and is in a lot of pain. He can hardly walk and he is trying to deal with the news while recovering. He has already signed the severance papers though. That's how he is. I know he would never want to fight over it or make anyone stay when they don't want to. But understandably he does want to know what has happened and why. He's been there from the start. We are – we were – a family. And now the girls aren't even returning his calls.

After Geri told me they'd sacked Simon, I had a whole week rehearsing ahead of recording *An Audience with the Spice Girls* at LWT the following weekend. It was going to be huge; they were expecting something like 12 million viewers. Unusually it was going to be a mostly female audience. Everyone from Sam Fox, the former Page Three model, to Lorraine Kelly was coming, and the girls were going to perform and answer questions about their lives.

They flew home on a private plane. At least while they were in the air I could contain the news. I took calls and went ahead with all the usual procedures in the run-up to a show like this as best I could. As soon as possible after they landed, Nick and I went to meet them at the rehearsal studios near the LWT building on the South Bank.

The studios were open-plan and faceless, like a big office block. They were all crammed into one corner of the dressing room when we found them, taking a break for something to eat. There were pizza boxes, half-eaten salads and cans of pop all over the place. As soon as we walked in the room Geri jumped up and hugged me and said: 'Nicki, we've done it, we're now officially looking after ourselves and he has agreed!', almost like I was meant to rejoice at the news.

Further explanations revealed that it wasn't only Simon they had dropped. They'd also said goodbye to drivers, assistants, everyone. Anyone they saw as Simon's people, they had removed. The ones they didn't let go left of their own accord. The girls said they want to manage themselves. Because, as Mel C offered from the back of the room, they feel they are unmanageable. I was dumbstruck. I stood looking at Geri who was only half made-up to look like Ginger Spice, the regular girl I know so well still visible under the painted-on eyebrows. I didn't want to give away too much but I could feel my head shaking in disbelief. I kept thinking about everyone I knew who was coming to watch *An Audience with the Spice Girls*. Could it even go ahead? They all seemed quite buoyant and oblivious – or at least in denial – to the magnitude of what they'd done.

'Is this really what you want?' I asked them.

Behind Geri, Emma was on the phone, looking quite stressed. She looks so different when she doesn't have the trademark baby bunches in. I realised she was talking to a taxi company, trying to set up an account and organise cars to get them home later. She was literally there with the phone book in her hand, calling A1 Taxis or whoever, telling the person on the other end her address. Someone's parents had already offered to run the fan club, apparently. I just couldn't believe what I was hearing. They didn't seem to have a clue about what they had done, the layers and layers of people and admin and work that go into making them tick. Then Mel B said: 'We still want you and Nick to look after us of course. It'll be us, Nicki and Nick. Just us and you.'

Emma stopped talking on the phone and they all looked at me in anticipation. Had it even occurred to them that I might not stick with them? Had they not realised that there's no way out of this situation where I would still be the Spice Girls' publicist?

'I'm sorry girls. We can't do that. I work with Simon. So does Nick. I wouldn't be here if it wasn't for him. I can't work with you any more. Please don't hate me.' It was so hard to say that. They have to do what's right for them, I understand and respect that. But equally I have to do what's right for me.

Sure, I had tossed the idea around in my mind, for the briefest of moments, of joining them. The Spice Girls are only going in one direction: up. Things can only get better, as the election anthem by D:Ream had promised us all just a few months ago, when Tony Blair and Labour came to power. They are a global juggernaut of stardom. And even though they have so rashly torn down the whole infrastructure of their success, it won't take them long to rebuild it. I love them. I love these girls. I know I could have an incredible time managing them and would enjoy all the perks along the way if I jump ship now. But I could only entertain that idea for a nanosecond. I am caught in a terrible family feud but, ultimately, I know where my loyalties lie. I can't do it to him. I wouldn't have had any of it without Simon Fuller. And as I always say, you should never make a career move for the money.

The tears began to spring from my eyes and the girls were all hugging me and I said: 'I'm so sorry, I don't want to leave you but he's one of my best friends. You need someone who isn't so emotionally involved to steer this ship now.'

And I walked away from them, from the biggest act in the world. I've spent most of this week calling up my contacts on television shows everywhere, explaining to them that I'm not looking after the girls any more. I've left in place all the confirmed appearances and performances that I have in the diary for them. I could easily have pulled them but I haven't. The world tour they've been planning is no longer my remit. And you know what? Everyone in television has been lovely. I hope it has helped that I have always been fair and honest. If I'd been the kind of publicist or manager who rubs people up the wrong way – an arsehole, I can think of a few – I think a lot of people would have gone around me to get to the Spice Girls and have them on their show regardless. But instead what happened is that almost all of my contacts said: 'OK Nicki, we're sorry to hear that. Who else have you got?'

A day later and Nick and I are landing in Rome. I've read my copy of *Vogue* front to back on the flight. Is it me or is this 'heroin chic' trend a bit worrying? Kate Moss is on the front in a blue sheath dress. She looks like a pencil, albeit a very beautiful one, but she has some colour in her face at least. Inside all the models have big dark under-eye circles and they all look so miserable. I don't get it. I think young girls deserve better role models than this. I also read an interesting article all about Nicola Horlick, the supposed 'superwoman' who has six children and a hugely stressful job at an investment firm. My God, it sounds utterly exhausting.

There was a limo waiting for us at the airport and now we are in the garden at Simon's villa having dinner with him under the lemon trees. It's good to be away from London and the fallout of the last few days. The speculation in the press about what has happened has been quite ugly at times and I am still heartbroken to have said goodbye. Nothing feels real yet. Some distance and perspective helps. Simon is still recovering from his surgery. It was a major operation and he needs significant rest, but he looks well in his white linen trousers and navy open-neck shirt. The truth is Simon does a lot of his work away from the mêlée. This is not the first time I've been summoned to a beautiful location to have a meeting with him. Much of the Spice Girls' success was planned on a beach in the South of France. He always says: 'When we're sitting together, Nicki, we get more out of each other, being together in one room for two or three days, than we ever would on the phone.' He is right, and I am not going to argue about going to Italy when I am asked to.

I tell Simon everything I know over dinner. Afterwards we are served the most delicious ice-cold *sgroppinos*, frozen cocktails made by his chef with lemons from the trees surrounding us. We've thrashed it all out and talked it over and agreed that there is not much anyone can do about the Spice Girls at this point. Polishing off his *sgroppino* with a spoon he says:

'So, are you ready?'

Nick and I say in unison: 'What for?'

'For our next project,' he says.

OK.

'It's called S Club 7. We are going to build a pop group from the bottom up and it's going to be called S Club 7. There's going to be seven of them. And I want you guys to go out and find them.' S Club 7, eh! Does the 'S' stand for Simon? I'm assuming so but I don't like to ask.

I have no idea if this new group will be a success. However, in this moment I know I have done the right thing standing by Simon and saying goodbye to the Spice Girls. His resilience and focus on new horizons is a valuable reminder that to survive in this game you need to keep looking forward and evolving. He has always been kind and considerate towards me, I think sometimes he sees me as his protégée. And I know that right now, when he's in a world of his own pain, physical and emotional, he's also helping Nick and me to push through and keep the faith with this new project. I know I will be forever indebted to him and that when you meet people like this in your life, it doesn't matter who they are or where they come from. It could be your best friend. It could be a relative. It could be someone you work with. Whoever they are, you hang on to them.

24

Because We Want To

'Tell us a bit about yourself. What are you hoping to get out of today?'

I think I've asked this question about fifty times already and it's not even lunchtime. Nick and I are running auditions for S Club 7 at the Lowry Hotel in Manchester. We put an ad in *The Stage* and let all the local producers and stage schools know about it. Thousands of young people have turned up to have a go. We've been schlepping up and down the country doing this for a few weeks now. It's not something you can delegate to someone else. It's proper, hard graft.

We are doing good old-fashioned auditions. They have to wait in a line and then come in one by one and sing a song before we ask them to talk about themselves. We put them through their paces with choreography, and they all have to go off in groups and do a number together, so we can see how they mingle and interact. Almost everyone we see is reasonably talented; that's why we've gone through the stage schools and young theatre groups. Otherwise we'd have everyone and their nan turning up. But it's not only about the talent. It's about whether they can function as part of a group. Together they need to have a bit of everything and not too much of anything. It's a balance.

We're also dealing with young people in their late teens, so I'm trying to get a sense of their resilience, how they might cope away from home, with long days and physically demanding rehearsals, and all the other challenges that come with fame. None of us wants to put anyone through to the next stages who might be going through other issues. Occasionally someone walks in and you know there is some-thing special about them. But mostly it takes time and more than one audition to know if you have someone who might make the cut.

When they don't make it we bring them all in en masse and tell them it's not their day. I try to be kind:

'Thank you so much for coming today. I'm sad to say that you haven't made it through, but don't give up, please, on your dreams, because that's so important. You might not have been right today, but you could be right tomorrow.'

There are a lot of tears, over-tired teenagers and dashed hopes. And a lot of pushy, but mostly well-meaning parents.

Equally, there are quite a lot of kids who turn up on their own. I have maximum respect for them. To be sixteen or seventeen and turn up on your own to stand up on stage and audition? I couldn't do it even now.

We're not only looking for singers. Simon wants S Club 7 to be a musical television show, with singing and dancing, kind of like The Monkees used to be back in the 60s, so they need to be able to act as well. There are going to be seven of them in the group so if one (or two) leave for any reason it's still a good bunch, like an actual club. He's seen with the Spice Girls how things can change literally overnight. People fall out and want to leave, maybe have families or pursue solo careers. So he's decided seven is the right number. The lucky number. The real genius part is that we can put the television show out around the world, and take S Club 7 international without them always having to be on the road touring.

I'm here to help Nick today as he is doing the lion's share of the auditions. It's all part of him taking a new direction. Neil Ferris has left Brilliant!. He was offered a job as the Managing Director of EMI. He came into the office one morning and said he was off and we could have Brilliant!. His departure prompted Nick and me to think about where we want the business to go. Artist management feels like a natural progression for both of us. It's what we've been semi-doing anyway for our different artists. Nick is especially passionate about it because he has been plugging a lot longer than I have; he's been ready for a new challenge for some time. Then Simon pitched S Club 7 to us. We're going to be working very closely with him on management and everything to do with the new band. It seemed like the perfect moment to push out into this area, so Nick and I have had some really honest conversations.

Over coffee on our little balcony in the office, Nick said: 'You know what, this is an opportunity for me and for us that we can have a go at. But it's a punt. We still need to pay the bills.'

As a result, we've decided we need the main heart of the company to continue. All the experience, reputation and contacts we have now put us in the perfect position to take on and nurture our own acts. But that will take time for us to build. It's a punt, as Nick says, and it's the promotions work that pays the bills. *Saturday Night Fever* is one of the highest-grossing productions in theatreland right now. At that first breakfast we had with him, Robert Stigwood asked our opinion on taking out some of the darker elements in the original story. We gave him our thoughts and it became a more family-friendly show, a celebration of disco. It's enormous, and we are doing all the promo. Plus, we have a team of about twelve people now, and the offices to run. Being responsible for other people's livelihoods is not something either of us takes lightly, so we've decided that for now I will continue to head up the promotions side of things while Nick develops our management portfolio, with plenty of back-up from me. When we get to a place with management where we feel comfortable, I can take my foot off the gas with promotions and put it on the gas with management, alongside Nick.

Nick and I have already taken on one artist: Billie Piper. Hugh Goldsmith, who I go way back with, is a personal friend of mine and Nick's. He called us up recently. He now runs a record label called Innocent, on which he has a girl group called Atomic Kitten, as well as Billie and a few other artists. He asked Nick and me to come over and meet Billie, because he said he needs our help. She's already had quite a big hit on Hugh's label with a great track, 'Because We Want To'. Hugh signed her at fourteen or fifteen – she left home to go to Sylvia Young's stage school at twelve years old. She's certainly a gifted performer. But working with young artists isn't always easy.

Now Billie is seventeen and he feels she needs someone to help guide her in the right direction and look after her. He said: 'Guys, I need somebody that can steer this ship, because she needs people who know what they're doing and have an understanding of the music industry. People who will have her wellbeing at heart.' What he also meant, but didn't say, was that she needs a woman on her team.

My immediate reaction was that we're not going to work with her until she is eighteen. But when we met her it felt like we needed to take her on. Billie explained that her father manages her at the moment, and said to us: 'I just want my father to be my father, and my manager to be my manager.' It felt a little bit like a cry for help to be honest, so we decided to answer the call.

She is already living by herself, or rather with her boyfriend Ritchie, who is in the boy band 5ive. Funnily enough Simon Cowell asked me to do the plugging for 5ive a while back; they even sent me a lovely card to ask me to work with them. That was so sweet – no one has ever done that before. But I turned them down. I wasn't sure about them: the music and the A&R direction is superb, but just not for me. Billie and Ritchie seem to have quite a tumultuous relationship, and the poor girl gets a lot of hate from his fans simply for being his girlfriend. Hate mail gets sent to her parents' address too. People call up and leave awful, abusive messages. She was actually booed off while she was performing at the Smash Hits Poll Winners Party. Ronan Keating and the girls from B*Witched gave her a hug. It's a lot for a seventeen-year-old to handle. To be fair, I couldn't cope with that level of scrutiny and judgement, and I'm older than her.

In one of our very first meetings with her at the Innocent office she left the room to take a call from Ritchie. I could see her through the glass walls in the next office looking increasingly upset, so I went out to see if she was OK. When I popped my head round the door, she beckoned me in. Obviously I could only hear her side, but she was crying on the phone, very distressed. I wanted to say to her 'Put the phone down.' It turned out they were breaking up. She hung up and slid into my arms right there, and we sat on the floor for some time. She was crying her eyes out because she adored him. There's a fine line between being a supportive manager and getting involved in your artists' personal lives. Not for the last time, I had to bite my tongue.

Managing Billie has been a baptism of fire for us. She is working on a second album at the moment, doing lots of promo, and the press is after her full time; they can't get enough of her, though not always in a good way. They are all over her love life, where she goes and what she eats. A journalist actually asked her if she's still a virgin. Billie is not quite eighteen, for God's sake. Leave her private life alone. Of course, we've worked with other artists who attract that level of attention, but when you're managing someone it's different to only handling the promotion. They rely on you for everything, they can call you at any time. You feel responsible for them. You're their lawyer, their marketing director, their personal advisor and their accountant all rolled into one. At the same time you have to hold firm boundaries because you aren't their family or even their friend. Well, we are friends, but you know what I mean.

She is such a striking young woman, but like so many of us is worried about her size and shape. We know she restricts her eating, and we try to do as much as we can to make sure she eats well. I get Alistair from the office to take food around to her if I know she's at home. On a recent press trip, she ordered very little of anything to eat. I had to draw a line and say: 'For crying out loud, not on my watch.' Then recently she collapsed at a pub in Covent Garden and had to be carried out. On a Saturday-morning TV show she was desperately unwell behind the scenes, so we've arranged for her to go to a private hospital to recover and build her strength back up. It's also to give her a break from the press frenzy that follows her around. I feel for her: she can't go anywhere or do anything like a normal seventeen-year-old. I try to imagine what her life must be like, but being completely honest, no one knows what it is to stand in her shoes. From where I'm standing, they look bloody uncomfortable.

Working with Billie highlights an interesting paradox at the heart of my work, because while all of this is happening, Billie is also riding the crest of a wave. She loves what she does, and she needs proper artist management because we give her a structure that she might not have had before. A lot gets written and said about the workloads many young artists are carrying, but if you say to them: 'Do you want to stop the bus, take a two-year break? We think you should.' Most would flatly refuse.

It's a fact of life in this industry that we work eighteen-hour days and numerous weekends. Not only the artists but most of the people around them and those of us behind the scenes. But at least we don't have the media breathing down our necks. Whatever your role, there's is no such thing as time off in lieu. It's not always healthy, but it's also doing what we love. The hours are ferocious, but we wouldn't want to be anywhere else.

25

Don't Stop Moving

The doorbell rings and Shacky goes to answer it. It's the Chinese takeaway I've ordered for everyone. They'll all be here in a minute, I didn't realise the time. We've been watching the news, both utterly shocked by the death of Michael Hutchence in Australia. Pictures of a devastated Paula Yates and their little daughter are on every channel. It doesn't seem like five minutes since they met on *The Big Breakfast*. My phone is pinging with texts from people who knew him or worked with him, or asking if I know anything more about it. I don't. It's been a long time since I had anything much to do with Paula, or since I left Michael partying with Robbie in Berlin that time. It's just so sad.

I take a deep breath and bring my mind back to the business in hand. Dishing up a Chinese takeaway for seven teenagers and three adults: Simon's abroad so it's just me, Nick and Shacky. Poor love, he probably just wants to watch the *Match of the Day* highlights. Instead he's got a house full of excited soon-to-be-pop stars.

I've invited everyone around to celebrate and to help them get to know each other better. We've settled on the final line-up, locked it all down. This is the official S Club 7. But celebrating good news isn't like it was with Take That or the Spice Girls, I can't pop the champagne open with this lot; some of them aren't even eighteen yet. Instead I asked them what they like to eat and they all said Chinese, so here we are.

They arrive one by one. We've got Tina, Paul, Jon, Bradley, Hannah, Rachel and the final piece in the jigsaw, Jo. Rachel was the only one we didn't technically audition. Nick got chatting to her at the Sony offices one day – her mum works in the canteen there – and it turned out Rachel is a great singer. Sometimes things happen like that in this game, things you couldn't make up if you tried. Jon, the youngest, went to Sylvia Young's stage school, like Billie. Others have come via the Italia Conti School or the National Youth Music Theatre. They're all confident young performers, but what I like about the group we have settled on is that they aren't what some people call 'Stage School Johnnies'. They're all natural, lovely, bright young people who are really excited and want success.

They're also a real mix in terms of personalities and

talents. Jo is the one with the strongest voice by far; she'll be the lead vocalist. And Tina is the real dancer of the group. Everyone plays their part and they seem to gel well with each other. It's interesting to watch them getting to know each other this evening. They've met before of course, in auditions, but now they're all officially 'in' I will be paying close attention to how the dynamics shift. And I want to make sure we start as we mean to go on with a positive attitude around wellbeing. After everything we've learned with Billie and working more young people, it's something we take very seriously.

There's a lot of excitement and laughter in the room. The girls are all in the teenage fashion of the moment: baggy, low-waisted trousers and a tiny crop top to show as much midriff as possible. Belly-button piercings optional. The boys wear sleeveless muscle tops or open shirts, and their trousers are even baggier. For the first time I'm starting to feel the high-street styles are not necessarily aimed at me. I feel I am a bit too old for this look.

It's a relief to have the final line-up in the bag. We can start moving now. We've got so much planned for them. The first single is ready to go, a super-catchy number called 'Bring it All Back', written by trusted pop writers Eliot Kennedy and two of the band members from Dead or Alive. They wrote 'You Spin Me Round', one of the best tunes of all time. It's got something of the Jackson 5 sound about it; once you hear it you can't stop singing it. The song will also be the theme tune to the television show they'll be shooting soon for the BBC, *Miami 7*.

I've been working with Simon on the television show. Not writing it of course, but talking about what it will be like and the general feel of it as a show, what it needs to reflect for the band. It's classic Simon: we went to the BBC to pitch it, and as we were walking down the corridor to the room the meeting was happening in he whispered to me: 'Miami.'

'Eh?' I said.

'We'll shoot it all in Miami. I'll tell them it's all set in Miami, in Florida.'

That was how it all came to be set in Miami. Just like that. And what a great idea it was. Miami has a great vibe, it's so cool and colourful with all the art deco buildings. It has miles of stunning beaches and pretty much year-round sunshine. It's on the east coast so it's far easier for travel to and from Europe than LA. The show is about a band who are trying to make it big but find themselves working as entertainers in a bad hotel and face various challenges on their journey to success. But, like the song goes, they never give up. The BBC loved it immediately and signed up for a number of series.

I've been flying out to Miami and working on small video diaries with the individual band members already. I'm enjoying doing that. When someone sings a song or does a dance it's great but it's only one-dimensional. When you follow them with a camera over a period of time you can really get to know them. You can see their face when they try a Cuban Mojito for the first time or follow their reactions as they see all the Muscle Marys on the beach. There's a greater depth to it. I'd like to do more of it if I can.

Work is really opening up for me in that sense at the moment. I love working with our West End clients: *Saturday Night Fever, BoyBand* (by Peter Quilter) and *Dancing on Dangerous Ground. The Big Breakfast* is a huge show now – Chris Evans has made way for Denise van Outen and Johnny Vaughan and the house has had a tasteful makeover – and I'm working with them a lot, coming up with creative new ways to increase their viewer numbers. It helps that Malcolm, the account manager, is brilliant at his job and always manages to crack a few jokes even though he starts at 3 a.m. every day. Not an easy gig. Nick and I are fortunate to have a Brilliant! (excuse the pun) team working with us who are as passionate about the media as they are the music industry. Music is still my number one passion, but I like the variety I've got going on and the fresh energy that all the young performers bring.

The S Club guys are talking about the films and shows that inspired them as children. They all agree that *The Wizard of Oz* was the film they all loved to watch, especially at Christmas. It's the perfect moment to tell them my Liza Minnelli story. No amount of fresh-faced youth will ever outshine the pizazz of Liza Minnelli on the National Lottery show that time in 1996. It's one of those moments that still makes me laugh out loud to myself whenever I think about it.

At Brilliant! we have a long-standing retainer with EMI Records that means we handle the UK television and promo for many of their artists. I got the call that Liza Minnelli was releasing a new album, *Gently*, and would we help with the UK launch. The National Lottery had been going just a couple of years by then and had proven to be a great show for us to work, especially for the more family-friendly acts and numbers from the West End shows because it was usually on in the early evening. The scheduling of the Euro '96 football tournament meant it was on later on this occasion, but I still managed to get Liza on there to perform her new single. Winner, Chappers.

Liza had turned up with her new lover, David Gest, who worked with Michael Jackson for many years and, one could reasonably assume, also shared the same enthusiasm for plastic surgery as Jackson. She also had her toy dog under her arm and a cigarette on the go at all times. He and Liza were clearly madly in love and it was hard to prise the two apart during rehearsals. There had been a lot of quite graphic snogging going on all day and a lot of people not knowing where to look. We were at the BBC's Wood Lane studios, and Liza was called for a camera rehearsal so the guys could work out their shots. With any act like this, there are usually at least five cameras around them so that the producers can switch views during the performance.

Liza was in a fabulous, Pepto-Bismol pink outfit and huge pink earrings. She started to warm up, then suddenly stopped mid-song and called to me:

'Nicki darling!'

I dropped my Filofax and rushed over like I was a doctor at the scene of a cardiac arrest. Liza Minnelli needed me.

'The cameras, honey. They've all got red lights on them. I don't want all these cameras on me, I only have one. Just one at the front. I'm not doing multi-cameras.'

I explained that this was most unusual and the producers were unlikely to be happy with just one camera shot pointing straight at her face. A whole three minutes of just one angle can feel like a lifetime to the viewer. We need angles and aspects.

As I was explaining this to her I heard the chilling words: 'Nicki Chapman to the gallery, please. Nicki Chapman to the gallery.'

I went up and explained what the issue was. As expected, the production team said there was no way they were going to point only one camera at Liza Minnelli on *The National Lottery Live*. People would switch off with boredom.

I went up and down a few times, trying to get Liza to budge, but she refused. It was a stalemate and time was ticking by. For a moment I genuinely didn't know what I was going to do. I looked down from the gallery at Liza smooching with David in his black leather jacket, oblivious to the panic she was creating up above. Then it came to me.

'Tell the cameramen to switch their lights off.' The cameras could still run but Liza wouldn't know. She'd think they were off.

'Is that going to work?' asked the producer sceptically.

'It will have to.'

I told Liza that the cameras had all been turned off but would be in position anyway as a precaution. She went ahead with the song and all was going smoothly, until halfway through she stopped to tell everyone when the single was coming out, that it would be 'available at all good record shops' and how much it would cost. It was the cheesiest of plugs. On the BBC! Live! She obviously hadn't heard about the BBC's advertising rules, or if she had, didn't think they applied to her.

The song ended and once again the words boomed down from above: 'Nicki Chapman to the gallery please. Nicki Chapman to the gallery.' What a disaster.

It always makes me smile thinking about that episode. The conviction of Liza Minnelli that only her most flattering angles would be seen on television, And the ways in which we all, but especially me, got around her demands. I hope the S Club gang take note. Divas make great stories but rarely come out well in them.

26

Cars And Girls

'Hello! Why are you calling me so early?' It's Billie on the phone. I only saw her last night. Alarm bells are already ringing.

'Nicki you've got to help me. Chris is outside. What should I do?' She is half serious and half giggling.

It's Saturday morning and I am where I usually am on a Saturday, in the office watching kids' TV. S Club 7 has gone crazy. The band picked up the award for Best Newcomer Act at the Brits earlier this year and their television series *Miami 7* and then *LA 7* have been unbelievably popular. I'm working on plans for a Christmas special (it's December but I'm looking at next year's special – that's how early Christmas starts in entertainment), a panto and a couple of other one-off specials for them. Busy is an understatement.

'What do you mean Chris is outside?' Who is Chris? To be honest I could do without any drama today. We did *TFI Friday* last night and it was a late finish. I left Billie to it. She was last seen at the bar with her pals and all the production team and Chris Evans.

'Wait, do you mean Chris Evans?'

'Yeah, he's outside. And oh my God, Nicki, he's bought me a car. A Ferrari.'

'He's bought you a car?' I repeat. 'Why has he bought you a car?'

I can't compute what she is telling me. She says he's standing outside leaning on a silver Ferrari that's full of roses and there are photographers snapping him and he's just waiting there.

'I'm not even dressed yet, I've only just got up,' she says. As though that is the most troubling part of this situation.

'Do not open the door.' It's an order. She knows I mean it. The car is one thing but the snappers are the worry to me. They are hounding her day and night at the moment. (Coincidentally, *Day and Night* is also the name of her single. I cried when it reached number 1, our first act as management.) How did they get there?

'Stay inside and leave the car where it is. I'm sending Alistair round now.'

Alistair is one of our team, a management assistant who looks after Billie. Luckily he answers his phone – it's meant to be his day off – and he jumps in his car and heads over to her flat in north London. While he's on the way there I call her back.

'He's just posted a note through the door with the keys,' she says. 'It says I can sell the car if I don't want it and will I marry him!' She's in fits of laughter, squealing, with her pal who stayed over. I suppose I would be too if it were happening to me, but it's not and all I know is that I need to deal with this. She can't drive, so if she even gets in the car the press will have a field day. Oh, Billie.

I was really hoping to get home soon and have a nice afternoon at the new house with Shacky. We've finally bought somewhere together. Four bedrooms, so we can have our families stay. And it has a little garden that I'm mad about. I want to fill it with flowers. He was so right about going halves: it feels like it's ours now and not just mine. Teamwork. I should be busy nesting and instead I'm dealing with Chris Evans and his big romantic gestures.

Alistair calls: 'There's a problem with the car.'

'Alistair, seriously, just move the bloody thing. Just get rid of it. Put it in the underground car park.' I know there's one at her flat because it's where I park when I go to see her.

'No, it won't start, Nicki. I can't make it start.'

Deep breaths, Chappers.

'OK. Where is it from? Ask Chris, if he's still there.'

He isn't. A few minutes later I'm on the phone to the Ferrari dealership in Park Lane, asking them how we are meant to turn the immobiliser off. It turns out it's the handbrake; they have a different type of handbrake. Alistair knows his cars, but even he is flummoxed by this.

I suppose I should have seen this coming. Although I defy anyone to see a Ferrari full of roses coming! They had been getting on like a house on fire at the show though. It was fun to watch them, they obviously had a connection. In the interval they went behind a curtain and swapped tops. He had on her tight top and she was wearing his floral number. It was really funny and a joy to see Billie laughing. The split with Ritchie had been long and drawn out. She seemed so carefree in that moment, like a light had come on.

I hadn't seen Chris since that Spice Girls business either, so it was good to have a bit of laugh with him and draw a line under all of that. He's a brilliant broadcaster and I don't like unresolved issues of any kind, so the whole evening felt quite healing and positive. He invited me to go along for after-show drinks but I wanted to get home to my new house. Plus artists don't want their managers breathing down their necks all the time.

'You guys go. Have fun!' I said, naively believing they'd all have a few drinks and be home at a sensible time. Instead they all ended up in Stringfellows. What's the saying about working with children and animals? Except she isn't technically a child any more, she's eighteen years old.

Sports cars and strip joints couldn't be further away from the other young artists Nick and I are working at the moment.

I think one of my very favourite, and youngest, acts is

Charlotte Church. We've been working with her for a while now. She's another one I thought was too young at first – she was eleven years old when we first got the call from Paul Berger at Sony. Paul is the boss of the boss at Sony, he is the top dog. When he calls, you take it. We've been working with a few of his artists, Dana International for one, and we have a great working relationship.

He said this girl, Charlotte Church, had been spotted on *The Big Big Talent Show* presented by Jonathan Ross. Bizarrely she was on to present her aunt, Aunty Caroline, but obviously someone got wind of the fact that Charlotte could also sing and they had her do a little song before the aunt came on. The twist is, she's a full-blown soprano; she sang 'Pie Jesu' like a proper opera singer. I watched the footage. It was quite incongruous, this cheeky-looking but also extremely professional eleven-year-old singing that angelic classic on Jonathan Ross's talent show. Old Wossie was stunned, you could tell.

A manager, Jonathan Shalit, had been watching the show at the time, and he got in his car in the middle of the night and drove to Wales to find Charlotte. The story goes that he found Charlotte and said he was going to make her a star. Like a real-life fairy tale. He took her to Sony and met Paul, and that's when Paul called us.

'Right, I've got an act for you, Nicki, that you're going to work.' He's never one to mince his words, Paul. But he is el Presidenté at Sony, so I guess he's allowed.

'She's called Charlotte Church and she's eleven years old and she literally has the voice of an angel. I want you to break her.'

My immediate reply was a hard 'no way'. 'I've worked with some young artists in my time, but I don't think it's for me, Paul. She's extremely young, for one thing, not even a teenager. And I don't think it's really my area, classical, opera, not my forte. I'm more into pop!'

'No, you're not listening to me, Nicki. You're going to work Charlotte Church.' I got the sense that, as with Billie and Hugh Goldsmith, Paul knew he needed a woman to handle this artist. He just wasn't asking very tactfully.

It was clear I wasn't getting out of it any time soon. But there is something about dealing with straight-talking people like Paul that is very clarifying and liberating in business. He wanted something from me so I asked for something in return. I said: 'OK Paul. I'll do it, for you, but I want to have free rein. I'm not having you telling me what I can and can't do, how to promote my artists. OK?'

'OK,' he said.

I went away and listened to her cassette, to the incredible, womanly operatic voice coming out of the speaker at me. I went and played it to Nick and he said: 'My God. She's how old?'

So off I went to Cardiff with Jonathan to meet Charlotte and her mum Maria and dad James, and her nan. Charlotte was still in her school uniform, she'd only just got home.

They are a lovely family, very much in awe of the attention they were getting and with only the best intentions for their daughter. I warmed to them all instantly.

They were doing up the house at the time. They bought it as a fixer-upper to sell on, so there were ladders and buckets all over the place. There in the front room, with the wallpaper half scraped off the wall, Charlotte sang for us and was just sensational.

Driving back to London I reflected on the best way to honour not only Charlotte's talent but her young age. The last thing I wanted any of us to do was to take over her childhood with this. The obvious route would be to put her on popular adult shows like *Songs of Praise* and *Wogan*. But I didn't want to truss her up as a novelty for adults to gawp at. I wanted her to sing for children because she was also a child. She is also hugely likeable and approachable. I knew kids would relate to her, even if they didn't know any classical music. She could show them what an eleven-year-old can achieve. Plenty of adults watch *Blue Peter* and kids' TV anyway.

So I went off and talked to all of the children's shows. My pitch was something along the lines of: 'I know "Pie Jesu" isn't what you'd normally have on your show but she's eleven, your audience are eleven, and this is something refreshing and different for them.' I figure so many kids are in school choirs and drama groups – I know I was. Here was someone like them who was out there living the dream.

That's what I've been doing with her ever since. She has been on *Songs of Praise* a few times now, but she has so much personality, she's at home in the spotlight. I can see her having a career in broadcasting one day, she's such a natural.

One of the most rewarding aspects of working with this most unusual of my acts has been the response I've had from the television producers I work with. From *Motormouth* to *Going Live!*, everyone has been so supportive and enthusiastic about welcoming her. Not only for Charlotte, but for me. I suppose it makes me feel that I am now well enough established, and trusted by the producers of television shows, that they welcome my artists without hesitation. Charlotte's success makes me realise how far I have come.

27

Stronger Than Me

'You've got to meet my friend Amy, she's insane.' Tyler's been nagging us to listen to this Amy's cassette for a while.

He's a young fella we've signed here at Brilliant! on a development contract. He went to Sylvia Young's stage school as well. (Say what you like about Sylvia Young, she definitely spots and nurtures new talent. Watch any West End show or television programme and one of Sylvia's former charges will almost certainly be starring in it.) He needs work but has a beautiful voice and could be great with the right direction. Nick and I have been looking for a boy and girl act to manage, a duo. There's no one out there doing it well and we think there's a real opportunity for the right act. Tyler could be the boy. Now we just need the girl.

Tyler's always hanging around in the office. I think he

likes to be near to where it all happens. We give him jobs to do here and there; currently he's backing up all our files in case this Y2K crash happens. I can't imagine it will, but if it does it will be a catastrophe. Tyler's got real knowledge about the music industry and who signed to what label when and all of that, so he's also very handy in the pop quiz at work. He's always raving about his pal Amy so we've said OK, we'll give her a listen.

He plays us her cassette and it turns out he's not wrong. This girl has an interesting sound – more like a jazz singer, though, than a pop artist.

'Get her to come in then, Tyler.'

When she comes in it's hard to reconcile the small, delicate girl in front of us with the big, wise voice we've heard on cassette. She plays a guitar – not very well, it has to be said – and sings us a song she's written herself called 'Estrogenius'. It's something to do with hormones and being a woman. It's not great, but it's good enough that you get the sense there's a real artist at work here, not just a good singer.

She's only sixteen, quite quiet; no ego about her at all. In fact you could almost go as far as to say she doesn't seem that bothered about whether we can help her or not. It turns out she knows all about jazz, she's got an encyclopaedic knowledge of all the legendary singers and writers. She was even quite rude about the Spice Girls. 'Bleh, can't stand them.' I don't think she realised we broke them. Or maybe she did and she didn't care. She says 'girl power' to her is about torch singers like Billie Holiday and Nina Simone. She's refreshingly opinionated for someone so young.

I don't know much about her background, but it doesn't sound like her parents are particularly involved. I know she still lives with her mum. Amy even asked us if we had a part-time job for her at Brilliant!. After brief consideration we said no. Something about her made me feel like office admin was not going to be her forte.

Because she's still only sixteen we've put her on a development deal like Tyler. They get a small monthly retainer from us, not much at all, but we give them time in the studio with writers and musicians and help them to develop their sound. We think a deal like this is a good way to work with young artists because they're not under any pressure.

I was telling Simon Fuller about her on the phone the other day. He said: 'She sounds interesting. Bring her over to 19. Bring Billie as well. Come on, you know it will be great.'

He's been saying he wants me to join him for some time now. We've worked so closely on S Club 7 these past couple of years. Developing that whole concept has been an extraordinary experience and I feel like it's something I want to do more of. Not only the music, but all the other aspects as well. Simon wants me to be his creative director. I imagine that I will join him at some point, but I feel very loyal to Nick, I don't want to leave him holding the Brilliant! baby.

Amy comes in most days now. We have two sofas in the middle of the office, my old stripey sofas from my first flat.

One's a sofa bed but I'm not telling anyone that – we'll end up with staff becoming lodgers. She comes in and hangs out and chats, asks us what we are all doing. There are shelves and shelves of records and CDs. I see her shock of black hair totter out to the back and she comes back with piles of music to take home and listen to.

I heard Nick giving her a talk the other day. He was saying: 'Amy, go out and live your life. Start writing, start working out who you are, do some collaborations with other artists.' He's already such a strong manager, I can see why he wants this. He is genuinely excited about this young, feisty girl. But with everything that has happened with Billie, we are both acutely aware of the responsibility we have for the young artists we manage. Nick is giving her plenty of space and time.

She's started producing some great new material, enough for her first album, *Frank*. Nick comes back into the office almost daily, all fired up because he's been at the studio with Amy and she's been working with so-and-so and writing this and that. Apparently Annie Lennox went down to see her play at the Cobden Club in Camden. Nick is gearing up to pitch her to the record companies and see if we can get her a deal. A lot of what she is writing is, I think, based on her dad and her relationship with him. She captures that difficult age and makes it something so many girls can relate to in one way or another. The great thing is we've been here with her from the start and watched her grow into a young woman who is now quite confident. I've got an image in my head of her at the last Brit Awards we were at. She came along with us and she's sitting on the lap of Serge from Kasabian, draped all over him and he's looking at us like: 'Who is this?' It was all done with humour; quite a funny girl she can be. Can hold her own with anyone. Although I do worry about her reliability sometimes. Last week she fell asleep in the departure lounge at Heathrow and missed her flight to LA. Nick had bought her business-class seats as well. She was meant to be doing a writing session over there but she obviously wasn't that bothered. Nick was absolutely mortified at the waste of time and money. The whole team wants success for Amy, we all believe in her because she's an authentic artist, but small cracks are beginning to appear.

He's certainly got his hands full with Amy but it's wonderful to see Nick taking this new direction, and to support him where I can. It kind of gives me itchy feet as well. I haven't told him yet but I've had a call from Nigel Lythgoe at ITV. He wants me to be a judge, or something like one, on a new talent show called *Popstars*. It's based on the search for a band, like the way we found S Club 7, only it would all be filmed and at the end the band would get a record deal. I'm not sure how I feel about working in television. Once a few years ago when I was at the BBC in Wood Lane pitching an act for the 'Broom Cupboard', a producer suggested I'd make a good television presenter. They said I should make a showreel but I had doubts that I could do it. I rang my mum to run it past her and she said: 'If you don't want to do it, darling, don't bother.' My mum is the least pushy showbiz mother ever. Besides, I loved what I was doing at the time too much.

But my interest is piqued, shall we say.

28

Left To My Own Devices

'We'll put together a band but do it as a television programme, like a documentary, from the start to the finished
product. I need industry insiders that have the credibility and
the experience to do it. Your name has come up a few times
already, Chappers.'

'Oh yeah? Who turned you down then?'

'Simon Cowell.'

Great.

'Never mind him. I need someone who's used to putting
bands together,' he says. 'Auditioning and all of that.'

I've known Nigel Lythgoe a long time. He's been the
Head of Entertainment and Comedy at London Weekend
Television for several years. I've worked with him on the *An
Audience with* . . . shows – the Spice Girls, Elton John – as well

as big productions like *The Royal Variety Show* and *Sunday Night at the London Palladium*. He's a big character, a magician when it comes to dealing with talent and a master creator of entertainment shows. Some of the UK's biggest family shows are under his remit. So when he calls, I listen.

Nigel explained it would be a documentary-style show following the whole process as we find the talent and put together a new band. The band will get a record deal at the end and the bonus would be that Nick and I will be their managers. It's a massive show that has already caught everyone's attention in Australia, says Nigel.

'My son and all his friends are obsessed with it. Interested?' he asks.

It takes me a moment for it to sink in but: 'Yes. Yes, I am.'

I figured I didn't have anything to lose. It's an extension of what I've already been doing with S Club 7, and another opportunity to find great talent for us at Brilliant!. Because that's what Nick and I want, to find artists we can manage. This is just another way of approaching it. I know from working with Robson and Jerome how television can help find and create stars in a completely different way. There's instant access to people; viewers form real bonds with the people they see on television. It's somehow so much more meaningful than simply watching them in a music video. It's up close and personal; moments viewers would never normally be privy to.

I've been concerned about what Nick will say but I don't know why, he's all for it.

'What a great way to find a new band! We'll get the best of the best. You'll be great. You should do it, Nicki. Don't worry about Brilliant!. See it as a sabbatical.'

A sabbatical would be nice but in reality it's more like a weekend job. The young people taking part in the show are at school, college or at work in the week, so we do the majority of the filming at weekends. There's me, Paul Adam, an A&R man from Polydor who bizarrely looks a bit like Simon Cowell from a certain angle, and Nigel. We're the industry experts searching for the band, and we've been filmed throughout the whole process from first-round auditions and boot camps through to announcing the final line-up and recording the first single and album.

We've been all over the UK, checking in to hotels on Friday night and up early for the auditions the next day. It's been an interesting process, especially working with Nigel. It's reminded me a little bit of working with Phil Smith all those years ago at MCA: the joy and the laughs of working with these strong characters. Nigel's approach is very different to mine; he can be quite brutal with the talent if he thinks they don't cut it. He was a successful dancer and choreographer. Having worked in the industry for so many years and risen to the top, he knows what he likes and doesn't mince his words. Sometimes it feels like we're in that movie *A Chorus Line*. It makes me gasp that he can be so blunt; I'm just not like that. I don't see any reason to be unkind, even if they're terrible. Although I have only seen rushes – the raw footage – so far, I know Nigel's approach will make good telly. Everyone loves a villain, right? I don't know what people will make of me. I'm not exactly famous, am I? I'm just that music industry woman, usually in my jeans and T-shirt with no make-up on. I wish there was more time to get camera-ready but I'm still running Brilliant! and looking after all our clients, so it's all quite rough and ready. Besides, in my mind I'm approaching this as an extension of my current role, certainly not a new career. I'm contributing as an experienced music exec.

Nigel has his fingers in many pies. He's responsible for some of the UK's most successful television programmes. As well as this show, he's the producer on *Gladiators, Ice Warriors, The Michael Barrymore Show, Blind Date*. We'll be sitting there having a full English in our old-timey hotel in Bournemouth and Michael Barrymore, say, will call up screaming at Nigel down the phone that he doesn't have enough exposure on ITV's autumn schedule or something like that. It's so close in many ways, a world full of performers and all their people, but also an entirely different universe to the music industry. But talent is talent, and often the demands on them, and us, are the same.

I've loved filming these shows because I've just been doing what I do, judging the talent and putting together a band. I haven't had to learn any new tricks or pretend to be anything or anyone else. Nigel wants Paul and I to be truly authentic music industry people and hasn't put any pressure on either

252

of us to glam up or do anything that feels unrealistic. It's taken a bit of getting used to, six cameras trailing us and being mic'd up every morning. It's an unusual experience having a soundie's hand up your blouse, but it's all done in the best possible taste. At the same time it's also been an education in the making of a documentary series. I've worked with plenty of television shows in the past but they're usually magazine-style, entertainment formats. This is a more fly-on-the-wall approach. No one is talking directly to the camera or hosting the show, so there's no pressure on me to deliver lines or anything like that. It's certainly not a scripted drama. It's about catching moments, capturing personalities, and allowing them to tell a story. It's like the little video diaries I do with S Club, I suppose, but on a far bigger scale.

I am constantly amazed, not only by the talent but the confidence these youngsters have. I certainly didn't have anything like it at their age. We try to make it as welcoming and friendly as we can for them. Paul and I are definitely good cops to Nigel's bad. But it's never just the three of us in that room. What viewers don't see is the production team who are also watching and filming the auditions. There are six cameras with operators spaced around the room, soundies with ten-foot-long poles and enormous mics on the end, their arms outstretched as they hover the boom above the contestant's head, trying to capture any nervous comments, whimpers, big sighs. Nerves manifest in so many different ways and it makes the viewing all the more riveting if you can feel the pressure and the determination these young hopefuls are feeling. There's also the coordinators, PAs and other assistants, all sitting out of shot for the cameras but definitely in the eyeline for the auditionees. A whole *Popstars* production family crams into that room and waits and watches. There's something almost gladiatorial about it, like a scene in a film when the competitor walks into the arena preparing to fight for their life. Change the century and the venue but the reactions and nerves are probably the same.

I try to always be kind, and make them feel at ease. I know how much hard work they have put in simply to be here. They've prepared their piece, rehearsed lines, memorised lyrics, probably changed their outfit at least ten times. We're hoping more young people will hear about this TV show and try their hand at chasing the dream and being part of something new. We've seen around five hundred so far. I've heard 'Reach for the Stars' more times than any human should have to. I think that song will haunt me for the rest of my life.

It's still a strange and slightly surreal experience. I've spent years working in television of course, but as a plugger, not part of a production team, and never on this side of the camera. I've always said I'm not one for the limelight, but I don't mind admitting I'm enjoying this experience. It's fun to be a newbie again, discovering so much about the way great television is made. I also like to think that after fourteen years in the business, I am a pretty good judge of character.

Being behind the table during those auditions makes me realise how much I've learned over the years, about performance and star quality, what works and what doesn't. Why a great vocal range isn't enough, and that you simply cannot manufacture talent.

Now we have the new band, Hear'Say. It seemed to come together very quickly. They're Danny Foster, Myleene Klass, Kym Marsh, Suzanne Shaw and Noel Sullivan. Five is still the magic number in pop (unless you're in S Club 7). They're signed to Paul at Polydor Records, and Nick and I will be doing their promo and management. Will the band be a success? I don't know. It has all happened at such a speed, the worry is the lack of time they've had together to gel as a band. And so much of their success will depend on the reaction from the public. But let's see. They're a talented bunch, that's for sure.

There was another chap, Darius Danesh, who made quite an impression on us but didn't make the cut. He's tall, good-looking and charismatic, with a tremendous voice and personality to match. But not right for our fivesome. We want a band, not a solo performer. But after his rendition of Britney's '. . . Baby One More Time' I don't think any of us judges, or the rest of the team, will forget Darius. In a weird way, it was my favourite performance ever, although I had my head down for most of it, pretending to make notes as I got a fit of the giggles. I'm sure he'll go on to great things.

I'll probably be away while *Popstars* is on in January next year anyway. S Club will be filming in LA and I know Simon wants to have some big planning sessions, hopefully somewhere sunny. To be honest, juggling my day job at Brilliant! and filming for *Popstars* has been pretty full-on. It will be good to get back to the people I work best with, Nick and Simon, and of course to see a bit more of Shacky. We've been like ships in the night these last couple of months.

But would I be lying if I said I haven't loved every second of making a television programme? Yes, I probably would. I've lived a life behind the lens, now I'm in front of it. Nicki Chapman: poacher turned gamekeeper.

29

Never Forget

Well, we did it. Brilliant! is no more. Nick and I have closed down the business and moved to 19 Entertainment with Simon Fuller. It's a testament to our fantastic team that they were all able to successfully get new jobs with the major labels in a matter of days, and it's reassuring to be told the Brilliant! name looked good on their CVs.

It all seemed to fall into place after a night out a few months ago. It was a case of the straw that broke, or slightly bent, this camel's back. Nick was still super busy with Amy – she's gathering momentum (and a reputation) as an artist and the buzz around her is extraordinary – and I was still running the day-to-day accounts at Brilliant!. I had taken a few of my team out along with a couple of new television producers I wanted us to try to build a relationship with.

Their company had some new shows in development that I thought sounded interesting.

I booked a table at Quo Vadis in Soho, a real institution and well located for drinks afterwards. I hadn't met the producers before and I was taken aback by how young they were when they arrived. There is no one I have more faith in than a young person who is ambitious and driven. But I also know what a tough job being a great television producer is. So many of the good ones I've worked with have come up through the ranks, learning their craft over many years from a young age. Producers need to be creative, inspiring and strong on communication and storytelling. They've usually got wicked a sense of humour and make an art of judging characters and measuring the moment. So much rests on their shoulders, they need to be across everything and everyone, it requires nerves of steel and a level of experience that cannot be acquired overnight.

I decided not to dwell on the age of my guests. The meal was divine, as it always is at QV, and the wine was flowing. Afterwards we decided to head up to the Met Bar on Park Lane for a nightcap. It's slightly past its Cool Britannia heyday, when Jeremy Healy would DJ and the parties would go on till dawn (the advantage of being a hotel bar), but the Met Bar is known as one of London's best style bars and is still very much a 'celeb haunt', as the papers say. As we pulled up in our black cab we were greeted by the waiting paps who hang around there hoping to catch a juicy snap of a drunk model or pop star, either going in or falling out. I notice one of our producer guests is pretty hammered as she stumbles past the snappers. She was topping herself up a lot over dinner. Everyone did, but she was in her own super-league of topping up. We were shown to one of the red leather banquettes – the guys there know me as I've been a member since it opened – and ordered more drinks. All on the Brilliant! expense account of course. We were squashed up quite close together as the place was rammed, and everyone had to slightly shout to be heard above the music and chatter.

Then the conversation turned to my career. They all like hearing about the people I've worked with, or as I call it, fishing for gossip. What are 911 like? Do I know Robbie really well? What's Kylie like in real life? What's the weirdest situation I've been in? During the chat the drunk producer piped up with: 'Nicki, didn't you work with that awful band, Soap?' She started to really laugh, so much so that I thought she might throw her head back too far and flop off the end of the banquette. Soap is a Danish pop duo I buried – an industry term that means they hadn't made it, not a literal thing – a couple of years ago. They'd had a go but it hadn't happened. It's nothing new. Not every act I've worked with has gone on to global superstardom. As hard as I've tried. Why did she find that so hilarious? 'And Jimmy Ray, didn't you do him? Whatever happened to him? Ooh and Madison? Oh my God, do you remember them?' She continued to laugh to herself, or was it at my career? I was becoming increasingly narked by this woman, who clearly had zero respect for me. They all got more and more drunk, and no one seemed to care who was paying for it. The other one then said something sarcastic about one of my team, along the lines of 'don't give up the day job' and made a vulgar remark about sexual favours in return for promotion. I looked at these people – quite frankly a little bit entitled, drinking free champagne and enjoying themselves at my company's expense – and realised something quite refreshing: I don't have to do this. I do not need to be here with these people, going through the same old motions or justifying myself to them with a fake smile on my face.

As we were leaving – they were going on to somewhere in Shoreditch, on a Tuesday – one of the young producers grabbed my arm a little too tightly and whispered loudly in my ear: 'Can you get us any coke?'

'No I can't.' Enough. Meal ticket over. I jumped in my Addison Lee without saying goodbye and thought about what I was going to say to Nick tomorrow. It was time for me to move on.

The next morning I sat down with him and told him what had happened.

'I know it sounds petty but it's the last straw. It's not the only reason, there are lots of reasons, but this is the final straw really. The catalyst. They were taking the piss. It feels like we are working harder and harder for the same result with all these new shows. I just wanted them to have some respect for our company and our people.' I put my coffee down and looked at him.

Nick remained silent.

'It's yours Nick, you can have it. I can't do it any more. I need something new,' I added.

'Don't be so stupid,' he said. I took a deep breath, preparing to dig my heels in. I felt so sure it was time to go but that he would try to persuade me to stay.

'You're my dear friend, and a consummate professional, Nicki, the best at your job. No one gets near you. I'm not doing it without you.'

I felt the tears coming. The relief! I didn't want to leave him, but equally I didn't want to force him to give up what we'd created.

'I totally get it,' he said. 'I was where you are about three years ago. But I've had Amy and Billie to distract me. Let's do it. On to the next challenge.'

It was like that bit at the end of *Thelma & Louise*, when they drive off the cliff holding hands. We both had no idea what would happen next but there was no going back, either. I'm a Capricorn, we're not meant to be risk-takers, but here I go again, walking away from a successful and financially secure business because of a gut feel. I've still never made a career move based on money and I'm not going to start now. My instincts are screaming out for a change.

As soon as we let it be known in the industry that we were

going to close the company, the drums started working and quite a few people got in touch to offer us positions. MTV and VH1 both reached out. Simon Cowell offered me a role at his record label. But it would have been the same thing, different offices. I think we both knew that we were always going to go over to Simon Fuller at 19. I felt the pull and knew by then that I wanted to work in television, to be part of the creative process and start making the programmes instead of only pitching to them. I would have the freedom to do that at 19 because it's such an enormous brand. The 19 umbrella covers television, music, sport and film. The possibilities are vast and Simon wants me on board.

Now Nick and I have offices across the hall from each other. I'm the new Creative Director at 19, and Nick has joined the company in a kind of joint venture management set-up. He's brought Billie, Tyler and Amy over. What a starting roster for him.

30

Anything Is Possible

I've been in Malaysia with Simon for a few weeks and it has turned out to be quite a special time, quite significant. Pivotal, you could say. We've decided that I'm not going to be able to commit to managing Hear'Say with the demands of my new role at 19, and that the band would be better off being managed by someone else. (In a funny twist of fate, it looks like their new manager will be Chris Herbert, who put together the Spice Girls all those years ago. It's a small world but I wouldn't want to have to paint it, as the saying goes.)

Popstars is behind me and here I am, sitting on the beach in Malaysia with Simon and his brother Kim. A new chapter, a new direction, fresh goals and challenges, plus a very different office environment! Seriously, pass the sun cream. Simon has booked us our own magical villa looking straight out to sea. It's literally a short stroll in my flip-flops to the beach. It beats my old daily commute on the District Line. Talk about tropical paradise, it's as far removed from the offices in Acton as you can possibly get. It's exactly what I need after the last few months on the road working long hours, staying in crappy hotels, and the stress of closing up Brilliant!. I have to say I am feeling very, very relaxed.

Simon hasn't told me much about this trip. To be honest, he had me at 'don't forget your hat and sun cream'. Over fresh fruit at breakfast he explains we have an exciting couple of years ahead of us at 19 and this trip is our creative workshop to kick it all off. My kind of workshop.

Simon Fuller is a very relaxed, laid-back chap, but underneath the enigmatic surface his mind never stops – he's constantly turning over new ideas and concepts for shows and acts. He has a black leather folder he carries everywhere with him. It's full of notes and pieces of paper where he has jotted down projects, TV treatments, thoughts and observations. This morning he talks me through an idea for a programme he's got, called *Star Search*. It would be a talent show, he says, not the same as *Popstars*, because this time the aim would be to find one star, an idol, not create a whole group. And, 'here comes the secret ingredient, Nicki, the public will decide who wins'. It will be more like an old-fashioned talent show, he says, with performances and judges and knockout stages. But crucially the public will have the final vote, not the judges. The charts right now are dominated by Robbie, Eminem, Britney, NSYNC, Linkin Park, Steps and Westlife. Could an undiscovered act from *Star Search* give them all a run for their money? That's the aim, that's the dream.

I'm instantly sold on this idea, it sounds like the perfect way to find one iconic act from thousands of real-life hopefuls, and far simpler than putting together a whole band and all the politics that goes with it. We discuss who the possible judges should be. We need three or four pop-music big guns. Simon Cowell's name gets mentioned, the same Simon Cowell who the year before had turned down the opportunity to be on *Popstars* and told me he'd been kicking himself ever since. I don't think he'd want to miss out on the opportunity this time. And possibly Pete Waterman, says Simon. Maybe Neil Fox, for the media/radio play side of things. And the winner would be managed by us both at 19 Entertainment. It sounds similar to *Popstars* but different enough for it to be fresh. No one knows if *Popstars* will grab the public's attention or run to a second series anyway. It is actually being broadcast while I'm away, sitting here on the beach, so I have no idea if anyone is watching it. I do ponder on what the future may hold. Those couple of months filming *Popstars* seem like a fever dream now.

My birthday is coming up and Simon decides on the spur of the moment that we should fly back to the UK via Hong Kong, so we can celebrate my special day and also put in a few key meetings with MTV and some Chinese broadcasters.

It means not seeing Shacky on my birthday and extending the trip, but it's part and parcel of the job. Someone's got to do it! Simon – the man does have such impeccable taste – has bought me the most beautiful Gucci handbag to say thank you for everything and welcome to the company. God, if this is the future, I'm in. I'm thirty-four, I've spent the last decade and then some in the music industry. My new handbag and I are ready for the next chapter. I did mention somewhere along the line that I can be incredibly fickle, didn't I?

Dinner is at the Peninsula Hotel, one of the oldest (and swishest) hotels in Hong Kong, known in the world of luxury travel as the Grande Dame of the Far East. It's definitely an upgrade on the hotels I've been staying in while filming *Popstars*. We sit and watch the Star Ferry taking the busy people of Hong Kong across the water between Kowloon and Hong Kong Island. The harbour is glistening in rainbow colours as the lights from the high-rise buildings are reflected on the water. Simon says we need a nightcap, to finish off what has to be the ultimate work trip. But it isn't over quite yet. As we raise our glasses (Baileys on ice for me) Simon has two more nuggets to share before we turn in for the night. He's decided this brand-new programme he called *Star Search* the other day should be renamed. He says it's going to be called *Pop Idol* instead. And the final piece of the jigsaw: he wants me to be a judge. I gulp my Baileys down in shock. I'm absolutely speechless. Being a judge on *Popstars* was, I thought, a one-off. An incredible opportunity and experience, but not something I'd ever be able to repeat. To be asked to do it all over again, this time potentially on a much grander scale? It's honestly a dream come true.

I'm desperate to get back to the hotel room so I can talk to Shacky. We've exchanged a few texts and emails while I've been away but international calling is really patchy. The hotel landline is the best way to get a connection.

The line rings on and on and I'm just about to hang up when Shacky answers. It's late afternoon back in the UK and he's come out of a meeting to take my call on the landline.

'Hello! It's me! Can you hear me OK?' The line isn't great. 'Are you OK, love? You'll never guess what Simon's just told me.'

Through the crackle I can hear him saying, 'Nic, Nicki, listen. Have you not picked up your emails? I've been trying to get hold of you!'

'No, why? What's wrong? Has something happened? Are you OK?' All of a sudden, he feels a long way away.

'Listen darling, when you get home, whatever you do, don't walk out of the airport in your tracksuit. The show, *Popstars*, it's enormous. You're all over the papers. The whole country is talking about it. I thought you'd want to know in case the photographers are waiting for you. Love, everyone knows who you are.'

I'd left the UK a few weeks earlier as a music executive. I'm going home the girl off the telly, and my life will never be the same again.

Afterword

In spring 2019 I was diagnosed with a golf-ball-sized meningioma, otherwise known as a tumour, on my brain. Receiving that news was, without doubt, the most shocking and frightening experience of my life – even worse than being chased by an elephant on safari with the Spice Girls.

I am pleased to say that with excellent care from the NHS, my consultant and of course the unwavering love and support of my husband, family, friends and colleagues, I made it through. It was a life-changing experience, one that taught me so much about what's important to me, and that none of us can take anything for granted in this precious life.

In those dark moments during my treatment, when the future seemed so uncertain, I found myself reflecting on my past and the life I have led. I've always known that those crazy years I spent in the music industry were special to me. I was a young woman on an incredible adventure, my working weeks filled with joy, laughter, creativity, friend-ships, love and, of course, music. But looking back at them from a distance, in a pair of very stylish rose-tinted spectacles of course, I realised just how extraordinary some of my expe-riences during those years had been. Not only the stars and the talent I worked with but my career trajectory in that era, when the industry was still so dominated by men and when technology was ripping up the music business rule book. While I often talk about the career I had before I became a television presenter and broadcaster, I'd never written it all down. It began to feel important for me to record my expe-riences of that time, not only for me but for everyone who loves the pop music and culture of the nineties and early noughties.

People in the music industry writing their memoirs is not a new phenomenon. I think lots of people imagine the music business to be like the Wild West or, to cite Hunter S. Thompson (a quote often incorrectly attributed to being about the music biz when actually he was talking about the TV industry, don'tcha know!), a 'kind of cruel and shallow money trench [...] a long plastic hallway where thieves and pimps run free and good men die like dogs, for no good reason.' It makes me chuckle every time, although if you've read this far you'll know my time in the industry is not the usual tale of rock'n'roll excess. It's more about a music-mad young woman learning the plugger's craft from some true doyens of the business. It's also a story of a hard-working girl trying to make it in a time before Spotify and social media, before emails and voice notes, YouTube and Zoom.

And of course it's about a time of monumental cultural shifts. The political changes, the fashion, the move towards a more inclusive and diverse society, technology, feminism, environmental awareness and some of the most amazing music being produced across all genres. As a self-confessed pop tart it has been a special joy to spend time looking back and fully appreciating the importance of pop music and culture over those two decades or so, and feeling so grateful to have played a small part in it.

Keen-eyed readers may wonder about that chap who told me when I worked at MCA that I'd never make it. Well, I guess in my eyes I have. I'm proud of what I've achieved. (And guess what? Years later when our success at Brilliant! was at its height, he asked me for a job. Did I employ him? Did I, hell! I'm not always sweetness and light, you know.)

My music industry past has defined me beyond measure: without those years working with Phil Smith, Nick Godwyn and Simon Fuller, and the scores of other talented, crazy, wonderful people who have put their trust in me, placed their careers in my hands, worked alongside and supported and mentored me, I wouldn't be here typing the last few paragraphs of my book.

But as well as looking back, my brain tumour helped me to look towards my future. There's nothing like a life-threatening diagnosis to help focus the mind. What I want

271

most of all now is to be happy and healthy, doing what I love as a broadcaster and presenter, with the people I care about, who've been there for every version of me: Shacky, my family and my dearest friends. So I say thank you for reading my book, thank you for my health, and a massive thank you for the music.

Acknowledgements

Writing this book has put me back in touch with some fabulous old contacts. The early years of my time in the music industry were pre-social media, email accounts or phones that actually took photos. I know! It was really easy to lose touch, so these past six months or so have been wonderful, tracking down friends and former work colleagues. They've brought back more vivid memories than I could have hoped for and for that I'm truly grateful.

The book *process* has been both interesting and eye-opening – but they say that what doesn't kill you makes you stronger . . . I hope so!

So, to my team: Sarah, my literary shadow, who helped me when I couldn't get the words out, stopped me from waffling and was the perfect barometer of how interesting or funny the stories were. Sarah, thank you for your direction and being a fabulous listener. It would have been great to have known you in the 1990s – who knows, we could have shared some of these adventures together!

I have to credit the most patient man in the world, my literary agent, Kerr MacRae, who told me I had a story to tell many, many years ago – and never gave up. Sorry you lost out on our manuscript bet (who bets an electric scooter?), but your advice, support and patience has been unwavering. Thank you and maybe you can now talk to me about another one . . .

To everyone at my publishing company Little, Brown. From that first meeting about my memoir with Emily Barrett, who started the ball rolling and convinced me to do the book with them, to Cath Burke, Serena Brett, Kelly Ellis, Nithya Rae, Linda Silverman, Steph Melrose, Hannah Methuen and Caitriona Row – for all brilliantly steering me in the right direction with so much enthusiasm for my story, holding my hand and making it a joy. The publishing world is very different from music, TV and radio, and I mean that in a good way!

I'm indebted to my artists, who I've been fortunate enough to work with and many of whom feature in this book. To stand alongside Take That, one of the biggest British pop bands is really something. Then, to be fortunate enough to do it all again with the Spices, just incredible and certainly nothing I could ever have dreamed of. Without GB, Marky, Rob, Jason and Howard, I wouldn't have realised my ambition of travelling the world in the name of 'promotion' and truly learning my craft. (They taught me to always turn left on planes, not right.) Their humour, friendship and respect meant the world. It still does.

To those five mad, crazy girls who showed us all the true meaning of girl power. A dream to promote and who showed the 'biz and media how it should be done, always on their terms. The pinnacle for me being their day-to-day tour manager back in 2008. Thank you Ginger, Sporty, Baby, Scary and Posh. Love ya!

And now the acronyms! To the MCA family where it all started – Phil, Zoe, Freddo, Graham, TP, Liz, Andi, Miranda, Jeff, Rebecca and Greg. There were no better people to teach me what not to do . . . only kidding!!

All the RCA team in the early 90s. So many good people, so many memories, many of which didn't make the book for good reason – Thursday-night club anyone? Although I have to mention RP, Narrinder, Carys, Tam, Sammy and Erin, plus Jeremy (a brilliant MD) and Hugh.

Thankfully I found the best boss ever in Nick Godwyn, who became my dearest friend and business partner at Brilliant! Never on time but made me howl with laughter and taught me so much. A giant of a man. Much loved and respected and I probably don't tell him enough.

To Simon Fuller, who opened so many exciting doors. I count my lucky stars for that day at RCA Records when we first met . . . and more than thirty years later I'm still grateful for everything Simon has done for me, in front of and behind the camera. Without question. Little did I know how my life and career would change beyond measure. Standing by his side as Creative Director at 19 were some of the best years of my life. He saw strengths in me I didn't know I had . . . without him I wouldn't be a TV presenter or radio broadcaster. So many delicious memories – just a few I've touched on here. There will never be enough thank yous (but No More I Love Yous – geddit?)

It would be remiss not to credit all the wonderful and creative teams I've been lucky enough to work with since jumping off the music industry ship and diving into the world of TV and radio. People who put up with my stories even though they may have heard them more than once. Thank you to my Noel Gay family and the *Escape to the Country* team. To the researchers who politely remind me they auditioned for one of my shows (luckily, most say I was the nice judge) and, also, to the odd presenter who has finally forgiven me for not putting him in S Club Juniors. Sorry, Rylan. To Helen and all at BBC Radio 2. To think this is where it all started for me as a young plugger and, now, life has gone full circle and I'm back again. This time behind the mic.

I have to finish by thanking my family and friends – always supportive and enthusiastic – who've watched me progress from that nervous PA at MCA Records to someone on the telly and radio. They've often said I could talk and talk . . . perhaps, I've finally found my vocation.

Mum, Dad, Shelley, Mary, Graham, the Raptors; to my wonderful blended family, my stepbrothers and sisters; to the Shackleton clan; to my dearest friend from school, Krista, whose memory of those years is far better than mine; to Dr K, Rich$ & Bexy, Gabriella, Liz, Tim and all those I call dear. Or darling. Or every day!

Lastly, to my husband Shacky, who I love so much. It may have taken me a while to give in and say yes, but thank goodness your perseverance paid off and I wouldn't change a thing. Apart from Leeds United being relegated. Ever. x